THE
Princesses AND FRIENDS
VEGAN COOKBOOK

TABLE OF CONTENTS

INTRODUCTION

Hello and welcome to a magical wonderland of culinary feasts. Loved by so many, studios such as Princess Naoko Planning the studio which brought you Sailor Moon, as well as Disney, among many others have not only given us some of our favorite characters but also some of the most delicious meals inspired by each story.

In this cookbook, you will find easy-to-follow recipes that are not only healthier twists on the original meals from your favorite movies, shows and books but are completely vegan.

As you flip through the pages and embark on a magical culinary journey, you will find that taste and appearance don't need to be compromised for a guilt-free, dairy-free feast.

Designed for both adults and children alike, we hope you find as much joy in making these recipes as we did putting them together.

Bon Appetit!

SAILOR MOON
USAGI'S MOON PRINCESS GALAXY DONUTS

SERVES	METHOD	TIME
10	Oven	50 minutes

CHEF'S TIP:

*   *For an added magical sparkle to your doughnuts, add edible glitter stars or dust onto your gazed doughnuts before they dry.*

*   *Mix 1 Tbsp ground flax seed with 3 Tbsp of water to make one egg*

DOUGHNUTS

- ½ cup of dairy-free milk
- 1 tsp of apple cider vinegar
- 1 ½ cups of all-purpose flour
- 1 ½ cups of wholewheat flour
- ½ cup of cocoa powder
- ½ tbsp of baking powder
- ¼ tsp of table salt
- 2 flax eggs* see notes
- ½ cup of cooking oil
- 2 cups of coconut sugar
- 1 T vanilla extract
- 1 medium zucchini - finely grated
- 4 medium carrots - finely grated

GALAXY GLAZE

- 3 ounces of coconut oil (or regular cooking oil)
- 3 ounces of dairy free milk
- 3 ½ cups of granulated (powdered) sugar
- Food coloring (vegan option of your choice)

DIRECTIONS FOR DOUGHNUTS

1. Preheat the oven to 350 degrees Fahrenheit.

2. Combine the dairy free milk with the apple cider vinegar and set aside.

3. Combine the all-purpose flour, cocoa, soda, powder, and salt and sift through a sieve.

4. Whisk together the flax eggs, coconut oil, coconut sugar and vanilla extract in a separate bowl.

5. Using the sieve again, sift the dry ingredients into the wet mixture and stir until combined.

6. Add the grated carrot and zucchini and stir until combined.

7. Fill your donut pan with the mixture, ensuring each mould is halfway full.

8. Place in the oven for 20 minutes.

DIRECTIONS FOR GLAZE

1. Whisk the coconut oil and non dairy milk together until well combined.

2. Add the granulated sugar half a cup at a time and continue to whisk the mixture.

3. Decide how many different color donuts you would like and divide this mixture into that many individual bowls.

4. Using the sieve again, sift the dry ingredients into the wet mixture and stir until combined.

5. Add your chosen vegan coloring to each bowl.

CARDCAPTOR SAKURA
TOMOYO'S SUMMER STRAWBERRY SHORTCAKE

SERVES	METHOD	TIME
8	*Oven*	*25 minutes*

INGREDIENTS

FOR THE SHORTCAKE LAYERS:

- *3 cups of all-purpose flour*
- *2 cups of almond milk (or other dairy-free milk such as oat or soy milk)*
- *1 ½ cups of coconut sugar*
- *¾ cup of cooking oil (can be substituted with avocado oil for a healthier option)*
- *1 tablespoon of lemon juice*
- *1 tablespoon of vanilla extract*
- *1 teaspoon of baking soda*
- *1 teaspoon of baking powder*
- *1 teaspoon of table salt*

FOR THE CREAM FROSTING:

- *16 oz of dairy-free cream cheese*
- *2 cans of coconut cream (chilled)*
- *1 -2 lbs of fresh strawberries*

CHEF'S TIP:

The batter used for the cake layers can also be used in a cupcake baking tin to make strawberry shortcake cupcakes. (As in the photo)

DIRECTIONS

1 Preheat the oven to 350F/180C.

2 Using some coconut oil, grease the sides of three 8 inch baking tins. Using parchment paper, cut out rounds for the bottom of each tin and grease them too.

3 Combine two cups of milk with the lemon juice and place aside.

4 Combine all dry ingredients in a large mixing bowl. This includes the flour, coconut sugar, baking powder, baking soda & table salt.

5 Combine oil, vanilla extra, and milk mixture from step 3 together and gently whisk together until just mixed (and no longer).

6 Pour the batter from step 5 into your two baking tins evenly and place both tins in the centre of your oven for 20-30 minutes. Note: your cake layers are ready when a toothpick is placed into the centre and comes out clean.

7 While your cake layers are cooling down, beat the cream cheese in a large mixing bowl for 1-2 minutes. Add the two tins of chilled coconut cream and beat until peaks form.

8 Once your cake layers are completely cooled, layer your cake starting with 1 cake base, ⅓ of the whipped cream and 1 cup of strawberries. Repeat again twice more until all ingredients have been used.

CARDCAPTOR SAKURA
KERO'S "ALMOST PURIN" CARAMEL FLAN

SERVES
4

METHOD
Stove Top

TIME
*3 hours
15 minutes*

INGREDIENTS

FOR THE CARAMEL:

- ⅓ cup of brown sugar
- 1 tsp of water

FOR THE CUSTARD:

- 2 cups of coconut milk or soy milk (dependant on preference)
- 3 tbsp of agave or maple syrup
- 2 tsp of agar powder
- 1 tablespoon of vanilla extract
- Pinch of salt

CHEF'S TIPS

- *For a healthier version of the caramel, the brown sugar can be re-placed with coconut or date sugar.*

DIRECTIONS

1 Add the brown sugar and water to a small saucepan and bring to a simmer. Stir continuously. When this mixture starts to bubble and boil, turn the heat down so that the mixture can gently simmer.

2 Once the mixture has thickened, pour it into 4 ramekins evenly and set these to the side to cool.

3 Add all of the custard ingredients to a saucepan and place over medium heat while whisking gently. Now turn up the heat to bring this mixture to a boil. Reduce the heat once more and allow the mixture to simmer for 2 minutes.

4 Carefully pour this mixture into the ramekins over the caramel mixture. Refrigerate the ramekins for at least 3 hours or overnight.

5 To remove each caramel flan from its ramekin, use a knife to run along the edges and loosen the side. Place the top of a plate over as a cover over the ramekins and flip it over while holding the ramekins in place.

CHARLOTTE'S DREAMY CREAMY CHEESECAKE

INGREDIENTS

FOR THE MAGICAL CRUST:

1 ½ cups of crushed vegan graham crackers

5 tbsp of melted oil of your choice

¼ cups of granulated (powdered) sugar

FOR THE DELIGHTFUL FILLING:

4 packages if vegan cream cheese (8 ounces each)

1 can of coconut cream

1 ¼ cups of granulated (powdered) sugar

4 tbsp of cornstarch

2 tsp of vanilla extract

Juice from two small lemons

CHEF'S TIPS

* *Strawberries and blueberries are a delicious topper for this cheesecake.*

SERVES	METHOD
12 people	*Oven*

TIME	
5 hours 15 minutes	

DIRECTIONS

1 Preheat the oven to 350 degrees Fahrenheit.
Place two layers of aluminium foil in the inside of a 9 inch pan covering the bottom and sides.
Place a piece of baking paper on the bottom of the pan.

FOR THE MAGICAL CRUST:

2 Add the cracker crumbs, coconut oil and granulated sugar together in a mixing bowl. Once well combined, place the mixture into the pan and spread evenly. Press down firmly until you have an even layer across the bottom. Set aside.

FOR THE DELIGHTFUL FILLING:

3 Using a handheld or electric mixer, beat the cream cheese until it is smooth.

4 Add the remaining filling ingredients and mix again until smooth.

5 Pour the mixture over your prepared base.
Place your pan in the oven for 50 minutes, ensuring never to open the oven door. Remove from the oven and place aside to cool to room temperature.
Place the cheesecake in the refrigerator for 4 hours (or overnight). After this time, slice and serve with any additional toppings of your choice.

REVOLUTIONARY GIRL UTENA
ANTHY'S CANTARELLA AMARETTO COOKIES

INGREDIENTS

- 2 cups of almond flour
- 125g of granulated sugar
- ½ tsp baking powder
- 75 ml of chickpea brine (aquafaba)
- 15 ml of almond essence
- ½ vanilla essence

CHEF'S TIPS

- Amaretto liqueur can be added to the final cookie dough mixture to give the recipe an additional almond kick.

DIRECTIONS

1 Preheat the oven to 350 degrees Fahrenheit.

2 Mix the almond flour, baking powder and granulated sugar together in a large mixing bowl.

3 Place the chickpea brine into a clean mixing bowl and beat using an electric mixer until peaks form.

4 Continue beating the mixture until it no longer moves when you turn the bowl upside down.

5 Fold in two tablespoons of this mixture into the dry ingredients.

6 Add the vanilla and almond essence and mix well.

7 Create balls from this mixture and space them evenly on a baking tray lined with baking paper.
Bake for approximately 15 minutes depending on the strength of your oven.

TIME	METHOD	MAKES
30 minutes	Oven	15 Cookies

UTENA'S PINK POISON HOT CHOCOLATE

INGREDIENTS

- 2 cups of dairy free milk of your choice (almond, soy, oat etc)
- ½ cup of white chocolate (vegan)
- Pink food coloring
- Vegan whipped cream
- Toppings of your choice (sprinkles, mini marshmallows, chocolate flakes)

CHEF'S TIPS

Coconut milk is a great option of dairy free milk for this hot chocolate.

DIRECTIONS

1 Place the milk and vegan chocolate in a small saucepan on a gentle heat.

2 Keep stirring the mixture as the chocolate melts.

3 Add a few drops of the food colouring until the hot chocolate is the color you would like it.

4 Pour the mixture into a mug.

5 Add your desired toppings.

TIME		MAKES
10 minutes	Stove Top	2 Cups

STAR'S NARWHAL BLAST DOUGHNUTS

INGREDIENTS

FOR THE DONUTS:

- ½ cup of melted coconut oil or vegan butter
- 1 cup of brown sugar
- 1 cup of dairy free milk (soy, almond, oat)
- ½ tbsp of apple cider vinegar
- ½ tbsp of vanilla essence
- 2 flax eggs* see notes
- 2 cups of all-purpose flour
- 1 tbsp of baking powder
- Pinch of salt
- ¼ tsp of ground nutmeg

FOR THE CREAMY FROSTING:

- 2 cups of granulated sugar
- 1 ounce of dairy free milk ((soy, almond, oat)
- 1 tbsp of vanilla essence
- Pink of salt
- Pink & blue food coloring

DIRECTIONS

FOR THE DONUTS:

1. Preheat the oven to 350 degrees Fahrenheit.
2. Combine the coconut oil, milk, apple cider vinegar, vanilla extract, sugar and flax eggs in a saucepan.
3. Place on gentle heat and stir until the coconut oil melts and the sugar dissolves.
4. In a medium bowl, mix the flour, baking powder, salt and nutmeg together.
5. Mix both the wet and dry ingredients until well combined. Place the batter into a doughnut pan, filling each mould half way.
6. Bake for 15 to 20 minutes.
7. Take the tray out of the oven once you are happy it passes the toothpick test and allow to cool.

FOR THE CREAMY FROSTING:

1. Whisk all of the icing ingredients together using an electric or hand mixer.
2. Divide the icing into two separate bowls. Add blue food coloring to the one and pink food coloring to the other.

PUTTING IT ALL TOGETHER:

1. Cut off the wider rim of each of the cones.
2. Dip each doughnut into the blue icing and set aside.
3. Starting with the first doughnut you dipped, dip the edges of each donut in the pink icing.
4. Place the horn on the side of each doughnut, pushing it slightly into the surface of the doughnut.
5. Scatter your sprinkles of choice over each doughnut.

TIME	METHOD	SERVES
40 minutes	Oven	4 People

PRINCESS TURDINA'S TEMPEH TACOS

INGREDIENTS

- 6 corn tortilla
- 8 ounces of tempeh (broken into small pieces)
- 1 tsp of crushed garlic
- ¼ red onion
- 1 tbsp coconut oil
- 1 ½ tsp chilli powder
- 1 tsp cumin
- ½ tsp paprika
- ¼ tsp of oregano
- ¼ tsp cayenne
- ¼ crushed black pepper
- ½ tsp salt

EXTRA TOPPING IDEAS:
- Chopped tomatoes, guacamole, chopped peppers, vegan cheddar cheese, Tofutti vegan sour cream

DIRECTIONS

1. Place the coconut oil in a pan over medium heat and add the tempeh.

2. Add the onion and crushed garlic to the pan and cook until they become translucent.

3. Add all the spices to the pan together with ½ cup of water. Stir the mixture until all the pieces of tempeh are covered in spices and then cook until the water is absorbed by the tempeh.

4. Reduce the heat to your stove's lowest setting, stirring occasionally while you move onto the final steps.

5. Heat your tortillas in a medium sized skillet over a medium heat, heating each side for two minutes.

6. Dish spoonfuls of tempeh into each tortilla and add your favorite toppings.

CHEF'S TIPS

- *Serve this dish with vegan cream cheese to add a tangy twist.*

TIME	METHOD	SERVES
20 minutes	Stove Top	2 People

ECLIPSA'S "SNOOKER-DOODLE" BROWNIES

INGREDIENTS

- ⅓ cup of wholewheat flour
- ¼ cup of all-purpose flour
- ¾ cup of granulated sugar
- ⅔ cup of cocoa powder
- ½ tsp of baking powder
- Pinch of salt
- ⅓ cup of applesauce
- ⅓ cup of brewed coffee
- ¼ cup of cooking oil
- 1 tsp of vanilla extract
- ¾ cup of dark dairy free chocolate chips.

CHEF'S TIPS

- Serve these delicious brownies with your favorite vegan chocolate sauce and vegan ice cream for the perfect dessert.

DIRECTIONS

1. Preheat the oven to 350 degrees Fahrenheit.

2. Place baking paper at the bottom and sides of a 8x8 inch baking pan. Spray non-stick spray over the prepared pan and set aside.

3. Mix the all-purpose flour, wholewheat flour, sugar, cocoa powder, baking powder and salt together until well combined.

4. Add in the apple sauce, cooled coffee, cooking oil and vanilla essence and which together until well combined.

5. Fold in the chocolate chips.

6. Scoop the batter into the prepared pan and even out the top.

7. Bake the brownie mixture for 15 minutes, use a toothpick to poke the brownie and see if it comes out relatively clean. If it does, it is ready. If it is too gooey, leave it in the oven for several minutes longer—be sure not to overcook.

8. Serve warm or, place the brownies on a cooling rack for a least 1 hour before cutting even slices and serving.

TIME	METHOD	MAKES
1 hour 30 minutes	Oven	16 Brownies

INGREDIENTS

- ½ cup of popcorn kernels
- 1 ½ tbsp cooking oil
- 1 ½ tbsp Sriracha
- ¼ tsp of table salt
- Brown lunch bag with wax lining

EXTRA TOPPING IDEAS:

- A tablespoon of lime juice, chili powder for added spice

DIRECTIONS

1. Place the popcorn kernels inside the brown bag and fold the top of the bag closed.

2. Place the bag in the microwave for 3 minutes. Note that this time may vary based on the power of your microwave. One reliable way to know if your popcorn is ready is once the popping of the kernels starts to slow down. (About 2 seconds between every pop)

3. Mix the Sriracha, oil and salt together in a small bowl.

4. Place the popcorn in a serving bowl and drizzle the Sriracha mixture over the top.

TIME	METHOD	SERVES
10 minutes	Microwave	2 People

CHEF'S TIPS

Add a sprinkle of popcorn spice in your favorite flavor before serving.

INGREDIENTS

FOR THE CUPCAKES:

- ½ cup of brown sugar
- ¼ cup of vegan butter
- 1 tsp of ground nutmeg
- 1 tsp of vanilla extract
- 1 cup of all-purpose flour
- 1 tsp of baking powder
- ¼ tsp of salt

FOR THE CREAMY GLAZE:

- 1 cup of granulated sugar
- 1 ½ tbsp of dairy free milk (soy, almond, oat etc)
- 1 tbsp of maple syrup
- ½ teaspoon of vanilla essence
- 2 tbsp of your favorite sprinkles
- Several drops of vegan red food dye (until desired color is achieved)

MAKES
18 Cups

METHOD
Oven

TIME
40 minutes

DIRECTIONS

1 Preheat the oven to 350 degrees Fahrenheit.

2 Prepare a 18 mould muffin tin with muffin liners and non-stick spray.

3 Mix the sugar, butter, nutmeg and vanilla in a large mixing bowl until well combined. Add in the dairy free milk, flour, baking powder, and salt.

4 Fill each muffin liner ⅔ full with batter and bake for 12 - 15 minutes, ensuring it passes the toothpick test.

5 Place the muffins on a cooling rack for 20 minutes.

6 Whisk all the ingredients for the frosting together until a smooth mixture forms.

7 Once the muffins are completely cooled, drip the frosting over the top of each muffin. Allow the frosting to set before serving, and enjoy!

STEVEN'S FAVORITE COOKIE CAT ICE CREAM

How To Cook

DIRECTIONS

1 Mix the Flour, cocoa powder, baking soda and salt together. Cream the butter/oil, sugar and vanilla essence together in a large bowl.

2 Slowly add the flour mixture to the creamed butter mixture, ½ cup at a time.

3 Once both mixtures are combined and have a creamy texture, slowly add the water all the water.

4 Separate the mixture into two, making two balls. Wrap each in plastic and refrigerate for one hour.

5 Preheat the oven to 325 degrees Fahrenheit.

6 Place each dough ball between two sheets of baking paper and flatten them down and shape into a square. Use a rolling pin until the dough is ¼ inch thick.

7 Cut each of these pieces of dough using the Cookie Cat cutter and place them in the oven on a baking tray lined with baking paper.

8 Bake them for 6 minutes and then allow each one to completely cool.

9 Place scoops of ice-cream on the top of one of the cookie layers and spread it evenly. Place the second cookie layer on top.

10 Place your cookie cat into the freezer until ready to serve. Enjoy!

INGREDIENTS

- *1 litre of your favorite vegan ice-cream in any flavor.*
- *2 cups of all-purpose flour*
- *1 cup of cocoa powder*
- *½ tsp of baking soda*
- *1 tsp of salt*
- *1 cup of vegan butter or coconut oil at room temperature*
- *⅔ cup of powdered sugar*
- *1 tsp of vanilla essence*
- *4 - 5 Tbsp of water*

CHEF'S TIPS

After freezing your ice cream sandwich, let it stand at room temperature for 15 minutes before serving.

MAKES

18 Cookie Cats

METHOD

Oven

TIME

1 Hour 40 minutes

DAENERYS MOTHER OF DRAGONS AND DRAGON FRUIT SMOOTHIE

INGREDIENTS

- ½ cup of water
- ½ cup of freshly squeezed orange juice
- 3.5 ounces of frozen dragon fruit
- ½ cup of frozen blueberries
- Small piece of fresh ginger (to taste)
- 1 handful of baby spinach

DIRECTIONS

1 Using an electric blender, blend the water, orange juice, banana, dragon fruit, blueberries, ginger and spinach.

2 Blend until smooth and serve!

TIME	METHOD	SERVES
5 minutes	Blender	1 Person

CHEF'S TIPS

- If you would like more of a slushier type of drink, add ice before blending all the ingredients.

MINNIE'S BAKED MAC AND CHEESE

INGREDIENTS

- 2 cups of unsalted cashew nuts
- 1 packet of macaroni (16 ounces)
- 3 cups of dairy free milk
- 1 cup of nutritional yeast
- 2 tsp of salt
- 2 tsp of garlic powder
- 2 tsp of onion powder
- 2 tsp of dijon mustard
- ½ tsp of chilli flakes
- ½ teaspoon smoked paprika
- ½ cup of panko breadcrumbs
- 1 tbsp of vegan butter
- 1 tsp of thyme
- 1 cup shredded vegan cheddar cheese

CHEF'S TIPS

- Add mushrooms or tomatoes to the pasta mixture before baking for some additional flavour.

DIRECTIONS

1. Preheat the oven to 370 degrees Fahrenheit. Boil a large pot of water.

2. Place the cashew nuts into a small bowl and scoop over some of the boiling water over the cashews until they are covered.

3. Keep the cashews soaking until they become soft - approximately 15 minutes.

4. Place the pasta in the boiling water and cook for 7 - 10 minutes. The pasta does not need to be fully cooked as it will still be placed in the oven.

5. Mix all the spices together in a small bowl.

6. Place the drained cashews, spices, nutritional yeast and 2 cups of milk into a blender. Blend until creamy. Add the remaining cup of milk and blend again.

7. Pour the mixture over the pasta and place into an ovenproof dish. Mix in the first half cup of vegan cheese. Top with the remaining half cup of vegan cheese.

8. Heat the butter in a small saucepan over medium heat and add in the breadcrumbs. Pour this mixture over the macaroni,

TIME	METHOD	SERVES
30 minutes	Oven	8 People

CINDERELLA'S PUMPKIN BIPPITY-BOPPITY BREAD

How To Cook

DIRECTIONS

1 Preheat the oven to 350 degrees Fahrenheit.

2 Spray a loaf pan with non-stick spray.

3 Combine the flour, baking powder, baking soda, spices and salt in a large bowl.

4 In a separate bowl, mix together the oil, sugar, milk and vanilla essence.

5 Add the wet mixture to the dry mixture and include the pumpkin puree. Mix until just combined.

6 Pour the batter into the loaf pan and bake for 55 minutes.

7 Remove from the oven once the loaf passes the toothpick test. Place the pan on a cooling rack.

INGREDIENTS

1. 2 cups of all purpose flour
2. ½ cup of coconut sugar
3. 1 tsp of baking powder
4. 1 tsp of baking soda
5. ½ tsp of allspice
6. ½ tsp of cinnamon
7. Pinch of salt
8. 1 tsp of vanilla essence
9. ⅓ cup of dairy free milk
10. ⅓ cup of coconut oil (melted)
11. 1 can of pumpkin puree
12. ¼ cup of pumpkin seeds

MAKES
10 Slices

METHOD
Oven

TIME
1 Hour
5 minutes

CHEF'S TIPS

- *Serve the pumpkin bread slightly warmed and with your favorite vegan butter.*

MUSHU'S WAKE-UP CALL TEMPEH OVER CONGEE

INGREDIENTS

FOR THE CONGEE:

- ½ tbsp of sesame oil
- 1 cup of rice
- 1 tsp of minced garlic
- 8 cups of vegan vegetable broth

FOR THE TOPPINGS:

- 6 ounces of tempah cut into small cubes
- 1 tsp of paprika
- 1 tbsp of soy sauce
- ½ cup of cooked edamame beans
- 2 chopped red onions
- 2 small heads of sliced bok choy
- 1 tbsp of white sesame seeds
- 1 tsp of black sesame seeds
- 1 cup of bamboo shoots
- Sriracha sauce

DIRECTIONS

1. Place a medium pot on the stove and heat the sesame oil. Add the rice and garlic and cook for 2 minutes until the grains of rice start to brown.

2. Slowly add the vegetable broth and allow it time to boil.

3. Reduce the heat to bring the rice to a simmer. Cover the pot partially with a lid and simmer for 1 hour. Make sure to stir occasionally and add more broth if needed.

4. While the rice is simmering, heat sesame oil in a pan and add the cubes of tempeh, soy sauce and paprika powder. Allow the mixture to cook for 4 minutes until crispy.

5. To prepare the bok choy, Heat ½ tablespoon of water in a medium pan and add the bok choy.

6. Place a lid over the pan and steam the bok choy for 3 minutes. Season the bok choy with a drizzle of soy sauce.

Serve the congee with the tempeh toppings and drizzle with Sriracha.

TIME	METHOD	SERVES
1 Hour 10 Minutes	Stove Top	4 People

MULAN'S KICKIN' KUNG PAO CAULIFLOWER BITES

INGREDIENTS

FOR THE CAULIFLOWER:

- 5 tsp of cornstarch
- ½ cup of panko breadcrumbs
- 5 tbsp of water
- ½ tsp of cayenne peppers
- 2 tsp of soy sauce
- ¼ tsp of salt
- ¼ tsp of sesame oil
- 1 tsp of cooking oil
- 1 medium head of cauliflower chopped into florets

FOR THE KUNG PAO SAUCE:

- 1 tsp cooking oil
- 1 tsp of dried chillies
- 1 tsp of crushed peppercorns
- 2 tbsp of chopped cashews
- 2 tsp of crushed garlic
- 1 tsp of crushed ginger
- 2 tbsp of scallions

SAUCE MIX:

- 2 tsp soy sauce
- 2 tbsp rice vinegar
- 1 tsp rice wine
- 1 tbsp brown sugar
- 60 ml water
- 1 tsp cornstarch

DIRECTIONS

1. Preheat the oven to 425 degrees fahrenheit. Break up the head of cauliflower into florets and keep to the side.

2. Mix the remaining ingredients for the cauliflower together until a batter forms.

3. Dip the cauliflower heads into the batter and place on a tray prepared with parchment paper. Bake for 30 minutes.

4. To make the sauce, heat the oil in a pot over medium heat. Add the dried chillies and peppercorns.

5. Add the nuts, garlic and ginger and cook for 5 minutes.

6. Add the scallions and increase to a medium heat.

7. Mix all the ingredients for the sauce and add to the pan. Allow the mixture to boil and then reduce the heat to a simmer.

8. To serve, place the cauliflower heads in a shallow and wide bowl and drizzle the sauce over. Serve over white rice.

TIME	METHOD	SERVES
30 minutes	Oven	4 People

THE PRINCESS AND THE FROG
TIANA'S WORLD FAMOUS BEIGNETS

MAKES
24 Beignets

METHOD
Air Fryer or Oven

TIME
1 Hour 30 minutes

INGREDIENTS

FOR THE BAKING BLEND:
* *1 cup of Whole Earth Sweetener Baking Blend*
* *1 tsp cornstarch*

FOR THE PROOFING:
* *1 can of coconut milk (full fat)*
* *3 tbsp of powdered baking blend*
* *1 ½ tsp yeast*

FOR THE DOUGH:
* *2 tbsp coconut oil (melted)*
* *2 tablespoons aquafaba*
* *2 tsp vanilla essence*
* *3 cups of all-purpose flour*

FOR TOPPING:
* *½ cup icing sugar*

DIRECTIONS

1. Add the Whole Earth Baking Blend and cornstarch to a blender. Blend until smooth.

2. Warm up the coconut milk and add it to the blender with the sugar and yeast. Let the mixture stand for 10 minutes in order for the yeast to foam.

3. Remove the mixture from the blender and fold in the coconut oil, aquafaba and vanilla essence. Then add flour one cup at a time. Continue to knead to dough for another 5 minutes. Place the dough in a mixing bowl and cover with a clean towel.

4. Let the dough rise for 1 hour.

5. Sprinkle flour on a chopping board and flatten the dough on the board until it is ⅓ inch thick.

6. Cut into 24 squares and let them stand for 30 minutes.

7. Heat up an air fryer to 390 degrees Fahrenheit. Cook the beignets 3 to 6 at a time in the air fryer and cook for 3 minutes on each side until brown and crispy.

8. Sprinkle with icing sugar and serve.

CHEF'S TIPS:
If not making use of an air fryer, heat the oven to 350 degrees and place the beignets on a baking sheet prepared with baking paper. Bake for 15 minutes until brown and crispy.

41

THE PRINCESS AND THE FROG
TIANA'S CLASSIC VEGETABLE GUMBO

INGREDIENTS

- 2 tsp coconut oil
- 1 large yellow onion (diced)
- 1 lb okra - washed and cut into ¾ rounds
- ½ cup of corn
- 5 chopped roma tomatoes
- ½ chopped bell pepper
- 3 tsp minced garlic
- 1 ½ cups of vegetable broth
- ¼ tsp cayenne pepper
- Ground black pepper
- Cooked rice, quinoa or couscous

DIRECTIONS

1. Before preparing this dish, rinse and drain the okra. Allow it to completely dry before starting with the rest of the recipe.

2. Heat the oil in a large pot and add the onion and bell pepper. Saute until they soften.

3. Stir in the garlic and okra and fry for 2 to 3 minutes. Add the tomatoes and corn and mix well.

4. Pour in the vegetable broth and cayenne pepper.

5. Let the mixture simmer for 6 to 8 minutes uncovered.

6. Once all the vegetables are cooked, remove from the heat. Serve over rice and enjoy!

TIME	METHOD	SERVES
40 minutes	Stove Top	6 People

CHEF'S TIPS

- The bell peppers could be replaced with baby marrow, mini corn or any other of your favorite smaller vegetables.

THE PRINCESS AND THE FROG
LOTTIE'S CRISPY SOUTHERN FRIED "CHICKEN"

TIME	METHOD	SERVES
3 Hours	Stove Top	5 People

INGREDIENTS

- Cooking oil
- 1 can chickpeas
- 2 tbsp water
- 1 tsp bouillon powder
- 1 tbsp white wine vinegar
- 2 tsp onion powder
- 1 tsp garlic powder
- 50g tofu
- 200g wheat gluten

FOR COATING:

- 4 tbsp flour
- 200ml dairy free milk
- 1 tsp apple cider vinegar
- ½ tsp sriracha

FOR THE SPICED FLOUR:

- 1 cup all-purpose flour
- 3 tbsp cornstarch
- 2 tsp salt
- 2 tsp cajun spice
- ½ tsp ground black pepper

DIRECTIONS

1. Blend the chickpeas (and their water), water, bouillon powder, white wine vinegar, onion powder, garlic powder and tofu until smooth.
2. Combine the wheat gluten with the blended liquid. This should make a dough which is smooth and stretchy. Cover the mixing bowl with a clean cloth and leave to rest for 10 minutes.
3. Bread the dough into three even pieces and return two of them to the mixing bowl.
4. Take one piece of dough and slice it into 6 even pieces. Lay out a piece of baking paper and place the dough on top and to one side.
5. Fold the paper over to cover the dough and roll out the dough as thinly as possible.
6. Peel the dough off the baking paper and place it flat on a plate, brushing it with oil.
7. Repeat step 5 and place the layers of dough over each other with a thin layer of oil in between.
8. Once all 6 layers are complete, stretch the top layer and tuck it down and underneath the entire stack of layers. Repeat the above process with the other two pieces of dough.
9. Turn on your steamer and once boiling, place all three stacks of dough inside and steam for 90 minutes.
10. Remove the pieces from the steamer and allow to cool before placing in the fridge for 1 hour.
11. Remove the dough from the fridge and break it into smaller shreds of 'chicken'.
12. To make the 'egg' mixture, mix the flour, milk, vinegar and sriracha.
13. In a separate bowl, mix all of the spiced flour ingredients together.
14. Place a large frying pan on a high heat and add oil. Dunk each piece of 'chicken' into the 'egg' mixture followed by the flour mixture. Place each piece in the hot oil and fry the chicken for 4 minutes.
15. Serve while hot!

43

THE EVIL QUEEN'S SINFULLY DELICIOUS TAINTED APPLE FRITTERS

INGREDIENTS

FOR THE APPLE FRITTERS:

2 tbsp ground flax seeds

4 tbsp water

2 apples (variety of your choice)

2 tbsp lemon juice

2 tbsp vegan butter

150g dairy free milk

2 tbsp granulated sugar

195 g all-purpose flour

2 tsp baking powder

1 tsp ground cinnamon

½ tsp salt

Cooking oil

FOR THE GLAZE:

200g icing sugar

¼ tsp ground cinnamon

2 tbsp dairy free milk.

DIRECTIONS

1 Mix the flax seeds with water and put aside to let it thicken.

2 Chop up the apples and place in a mixing bowl with lemon juice.

3 In a separate bowl, mix the butter, milk and flax egg together.

4 In a third bowl, mix the sugar, flour, baking powder, spices and salt.

5 Add the butter mixture to the dry ingredients and mix until well combined and a batter forms. Add the apples to the mixture and place in the fridge.

6 In a medium sized saucepan, add an inch of oil and heat. Add a heaped spoon of batter to the oil and allow it to fry for 30 seconds until brown.

7 Remove the fritter from the oil and place on a paper towel to remove excess oil.

8 Once all the batter is cooked, allow the fritters to cool for 10 minutes before serving.

TIME	METHOD	SERVES
30 minutes	Stove Top	12 People

SNOW WHITE'S GOOSEBERRY AND RHUBARB PIE

TIME	METHOD	SERVES
1 hour 15 minutes	*Oven*	*4 People*

INGREDIENTS

FOR THE DOUGH:

3 cups whole wheat flour

½ tsp salt

¼ cup cold water

3 tablespoons brown sugar

1 cup coconut oil

FOR THE FILLING:

2 ½ cups gooseberries

1 ½ cups rhubarb

1 ½ cups brown sugar

4 tbsp tapioca

1 tsp cinnamon

CHEF'S TIPS

- *Serve with dairy free whipped cream or your favourite vegan ice cream.*

DIRECTIONS

1 Combine the flour, salt and sugar in a large bowl. Mix in the coconut oil and mix together until it looks like large crumbles.

2 Slowly add the water and mix into a dough.

3 Wrap the dough in plastic and put in the fridge for ½ an hour.

4 To make the filling, put ½ cup of the berries and ¼ cup of the rhubarb in a saucepan and crush them with the back of a spoon.

5 Add ½ cup of sugar and 3 tbsp of tapioca. Keep stirring and bring to the boil. Set aside.

6 Preheat the oven to 400 degrees Fahrenheit.

7 Place the remainder of the berries and rhubarb into a mixing bowl with the sugar and mix together. Add this mixture to the cooked berry mixture

8 Divide the dough mixture into two parts. Roll the first half into the pie pan. Prick the bottom surface with a toothpick.

9 Roll out the second piece of dough for the top of the pie. Place the berry filling into the pie pan and cover with the rolled out dough.

10 Cut small vents in the middle of the pie.

11 Place the pie in the oven for 35 minutes.

THE MAD HATTER'S LONDON FOG

INGREDIENTS

- 1 tbsp earl grey loose leaf tea OR 1 earl grey tea bag
- ¾ cup of boiling water
- ¾ cup of almond milk
- ½ tsp vanilla extract
- Sugar or sweetener to taste

DIRECTIONS

1. Place the tea bag in the boiling water and steep it for 5 minutes, covered, until the tea is strongly brewed. Covering the steeping tea helps to fully extract the flavors of the tea beautifully.

2. Pour the almond milk into a saucepan and bring to a simmer for 4 to 5 minutes while whisking vigorously.

3. When the milk starts to foam, add the vanilla essence.

4. When the tea is steeped, then strain the leaves or remove the tea bags.

5. Pour the walk milk into the strong tea and serve immediately.

TIME	METHOD	SERVES
10 minutes	Stove Top	1 Person

CHEF'S TIPS

- Sprinkle this treat with a pinch loose leaf earl grey before serving.

ALICE IN WONDERLAND
THE QUEEN OF HEARTS' CHERRY TARTS

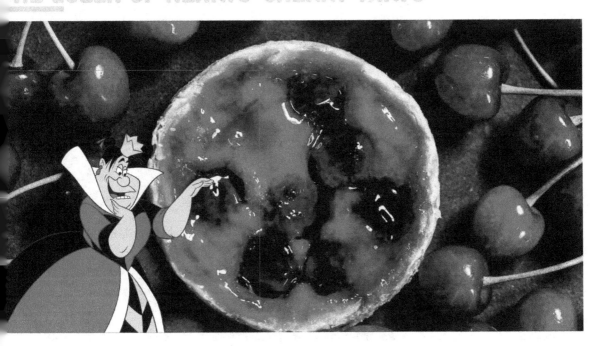

INGREDIENTS

- 1 packet of dairy free pastry
- 1 can of tart cherries (14 ounces)
- ¼ cup of brown sugar
- 1 ½ tbsp of cornstarch
- 1 tbsp of brandy (Optional)

CHEF'S TIPS

- Use cherry flavored brandy in this recipe to really enhance the flavor of tartlets.

DIRECTIONS

1 Preheat the oven to 400 degrees Fahrenheit.

2 Roll out the crust for the tartlets. Cut 24 rounds out of pastry using a 2 ½ inch mould cutter.

3 Spray a 24 miniature muffin tin with non-stick spray. Line each tart mould of the muffin tin with each of the pastry rounds.

4 Prick the bottom of each crust and bake for 5 minutes. Drain the cherries from their tin and save ½ a cup of the juice.

5 Whisk the sugar and cornstarch together in a saucepan on medium heat. Slowly add the cherry juice and brandy. Stir until smooth.

6 Let the mixture cook and thicken for 2 - 3 minutes. Once it is smooth and clear, it is ready and can be removed from heat. Stir in the cherries.

7 Spoon the cherry mixture into each of the moulds. Bake the tartlets for 8 - 10 minutes.

8 Serve the tartlets cooled to room temperature. Enjoy!

TIME	METHOD	MAKES
40 minutes	Oven	24 Tartlets

47

ALICE'S TOAST POINTS WITH SPINACH DIP

INGREDIENTS

FOR THE DIP:

- *1 packet of frozen/fresh chopped spinach*
- *1 dairy-free vegan sour cream*
- *1/2 cup egg-free mayonnaise*
- *1 packet onion soup mix*

FOR TOAST POINTS:

- *8 slices of wholewheat bread*
- *2 tbsp vegan butter*
- *Freshly ground black pepper*

CHEF'S TIPS

- This dip also pairs well with tortilla chips, or fresh cut dipping veggies (like carrots, celery and cucumber)

DIRECTIONS

FOR THE DIP:

1. If using frozen spinach, make sure it is thawed out completely and drained.

2. Combine the spinach, sour cream, mayonnaise and onion soup mix in a large mixing bowl.

3. For the best opportunity for these ingredients to marinate, place in the fridge overnight.

4. Before serving, add a dash of salt or your favorite hot sauce.

FOR THE TOAST POINTS:

5. Preheat the oven to 400 degrees fahrenheit.

6. Melt the butter in a small saucepan.

7. Cut the crusts off each slice of bread. Brush 1 side of each slide of bread with the butter mixture. Cut each slice of bread into 4 triangles.

8. Prepare a baking sheet with baking paper and place the bread on the pan with the buttered side facing up.

9. Bake for 6 - 8 minutes until the slices are crispy.

TIME	METHOD	SERVES
10 minutes	Stove Top / Oven	12 People

ALICE IN WONDERLAND

THE WHITE RABBIT'S FAVORITE GARDEN SALAD

INGREDIENTS

- 1 cup of cooked garden peas
- 1 small head of chopped lettuce
- 2 cups of chopped baby spinach
- 2 cups of chopped kale with their stems removed.
- 1 cup of chopped broccoli
- 1 green chopped apple
- 1 ripe avocado
- 1/2 cup of broccoli stems
- 2 limes
- 1 tbsp olive oil
- 2 tbsp apple cider vinegar
- 1/2 tsp salt
- 1/2 tsp oregano
- 1/2 tsp celery salt
- 1 cup of water

DIRECTIONS

1. Toss all of the ingredients in a large serving dish.

2. Drizzle the garden salad with your favorite salad dressing.

3. Serve and enjoy!

CHEF'S TIPS

- *Vinaigrettes are a delicious dressing to use on this salad. Try topping the salad with chopped walnuts, or pecans, or even flax seeds or poppy seeds.*

TIME
20 minutes

SERVES
2-4 People

49

MERIDA'S TRIPLETS SCOTTISH SWEET BUNS (ICED BUNS)

INGREDIENTS

100G OF VEGAN BUTTER

- 230g all-purpose flour
- 275g of dairy free yoghurt
- 2 ½ tsp baking powder
- ½ tsp xanthan gum
- 100g granulated sugar

FOR THE ICING:

- 200g icing sugar
- 1 tsp vanilla essence
- Your favourite sprinkles

DIRECTIONS

1. Preheat the oven to 350 degrees fahrenheit and grease a baking tray.

2. Mix the bun ingredients together in a bowl until you have a sticky dough.

3. Let the dough stand for 30 minutes.

4. Divide the dough into 100g balls and roll them into the shape of a bread roll.

5. Place each bun on the baking tray and in the oven for 25-30 minutes.

6. Remove them from the oven and set them aside to cool slightly.

7. Mix the icing ingredients together until you have a smooth and spreadable mixture.

8. Drip the icing on top of each role and add your favorite sprinkles.

TIME	METHOD	SERVES
40 minutes	Oven	5-6 People

CHEF'S TIPS

- *Forgo the sprinkles and top your sweet buns with a maraschino cherry to get the classic movie look*

50

MOANA'S HAUPIA CHOCOLATE COCONUT PIE

TIME	METHOD	SERVES
4 Hours 45 Minutes	Oven	10 People

INGREDIENTS

1 unbaked pie crust (dairy free)

1 can coconut cream

1 ¾ cups almond milk

⅔ cup brown sugar

1 tsp coconut essence

½ cup water

½ cup cornstarch

5 ounces dark chocolate (dairy free)

Whipped coconut cream

¼ cup coconut flakes

1 cup of dried beans

CHEF'S TIPS

Sprinkle grated vegan chocolate over the pie slices before serving. .

DIRECTIONS

1 Preheat the oven to 350 degrees fahrenheit.

2 Line the pie crust with baking paper and place the dried beans on top of the paper. Place the crust in the oven for 15 minutes to bake and then into the fridge to cool.

3 Whisk the coconut cream, milk, sugar and coconut essence together in a saucepan.

4 In a separate bowl, whisk the cornstarch and water together.

5 Place the milk mixture on the stove and bring to a boil followed by a simmering heat. Slowly add the cornstarch mixture and continue to whisk the mixture until it starts to thicken.

6 Place the chocolate in a small bowl and pour 1-2 cups of the milk mixture over. Whisk the mix together until the chocolate is melted and mixed in.

7 Pour the chocolate mixture into the pie crust and even it out.

8 Mix the milk mixture vigorously and pour on top of the chocolate mixture.

9 Place the pie in the fridge for 3 to 4 hours. When ready to serve, top the pie with whipped coconut and sprinkle with coconut flakes.

MOANA
MAUI'S BIG KAHUNA BURGERS

TIME	METHOD	SERVES
4 Hours 45 Minutes	Oven	10 People

CHEF'S TIP:

Butter your buns with a bit of vegan butter ot margerine, and toast the buns in the oven for 30 seconds to 1 minute before assembling to give our burger a crunchy exterior.

Looking for more toppings for this hearty burger? Try adding tempeh bacon or any other non-meat bacon. Hot peppers or jalapeno peppers make the perfect combination of spicy and sweet. You can also swap out lettuce for crunchy kale.

SERVES
5

METHOD
Oven

TIME
15 minutes

INGREDIENTS

FOR THE CHICKPEA PATTIES:

- *2 cans chickpeas*
- *½ cup walnuts*
- *½ cup corn*
- *½ cup oats*
- *¼ cup chopped onion*
- *1 ½ tbsp onion powder*
- *2 tsp garlic powder*
- *½ tsp smoked paprika*

HULI-HULI SAUCE:

- *½ cup of pineapple juice*
- *⅓ cup tamari*
- *⅓ cup coconut sugar*
- *2 tbsp ketchup*
- *1 tbsp cornstarch*
- *½ tsp garlic powder*

FOR SERVING:

- *8 burger buns*
- *Butter lettuce*
- *Chopped red onion*
- *Grilled pineapple rings*

DIRECTIONS

FOR THE CHICKPEA PATTIES:

1 *Place the walnuts, corn and oats in a blender or food processor until they are roughly chopped.*

2 *Add the remaining patty ingredients and pulse again until just combined.*

3 *Divide the patty mixture into 8 balls and shape the patties into your required thickness.*

4 *Cook the patties over medium heat for 5 minutes on each side. Add each patty to a burger bun with toppings and drizzle with Huli-Huli sauce.*

HULI-HULI SAUCE:

1 *Whisk all the ingredients together in a small saucepan and bring to a simmer over medium heat.*

2 *Continue to whisk the sauce until a glaze forms.*

3 *Taste the sauce and add additional pineapple juice to suit your preference.*

TAMATOA'S GOLDEN BATTERED 'FISH' TACOS

INGREDIENTS

- 1 - 2 packets of meat-free fish fillets
- 2 cups of shredded cabbage
- 1 ripe avocado
- ½ cup vegan sour cream
- ¼ cup of salsa
- Cilantro for garnish
- 12 Corn tortillas

DIRECTIONS

1 Cook the fish fillets according to the packaging. In a small bowl, mix the sour cream, ½ an avocado and salsa together.

2 Construct the tacos with the fish fillets, sour cream mix and cabbage.

3 Serve and enjoy!

TIME	METHOD	SERVES
30 minutes	Oven	6 People

CHEF'S TIPS

- Add sriracha to the sour cream mix to give your tacos a spicy kick.

MOANA'S TASTY TEMPEH WINGS

INGREDIENTS

FOR THE TEMPEH WINGS:

- 8 oz. tempeh
- ½ cup of orange juice
- 2 tbsp low sodium soy sauce
- ¼ cup water
- 1 tbsp rice wine vinegar
- ½ tsp grated ginger
- For the wing sauce:
- ¼ cup orange juice
- 1 tbsp low sodium soy sauce
- ¼ cup coconut sugar
- 1 ½ tsp cornstarch
- ½ tsp chilli sauce
- 1 tsp ginger, grated

CHEF'S TIPS

- Garnish the wings with thinly sliced green peppers before serving.

DIRECTIONS

1. The first step is to marinate the tempeh. Slice the tempeh into strips and place it into a mixing bowl.

2. Pour over the orange juice, water, soy sauce, rice wine vinegar and ginger into the bowl.

3. Make sure all of the tempeh is coated in the marinade and allow it to soak for 30 minutes.

4. Preheat the oven to 375 degrees Fahrenheit. Preheat a pan by lining it with baking paper and spraying it with nonstick spray.

5. Place the tempeh on the pan and bake for 10 to 15 minutes until the tempeh starts to brown and is firm on the outside.

6. Make the sauce while the tempeh is in the oven. Whisk all the sauce ingredients together in a small saucepan and place on medium heat. The sauce will take 3 to 5 minutes to thicken.

7. Place the wings from the oven into the sauce and make sure they are completely coated. Then put the wings back on the pan once again and in the oven for another 2 minutes.

8. Remove from the oven and serve.

TIME	METHOD	SERVES
60 minutes	Oven	2 People

OLAF'S BLUEBERRY YOGURT POPSICLES

INGREDIENTS

- 1 ½ cups frozen blueberries
- 1 can coconut cream
- 2 tbsp arrowroot powder
- 2 tbsp organic honey,
- 1 ½ tsp vanilla essence
- ⅛ tsp vanilla powder

DIRECTIONS

1. Whisk the coconut cream, arrowroot powder and honey together in a medium saucepan. Allow the mixture to simmer until it thickens.

2. Let the mixture cool and add in the vanilla essence and powder.

3. Pour 1 cup of the mixture into 8 popsicle molds, and fill ⅓ full. Freeze for about 1 hour.

4. Blend the blueberries with the remaining coconut cream mixture and blend for 30 seconds.

5. Pour the blueberry mixture into the popsicle moulds until each one is full. Freeze the popsicles for 6 hours before serving.

TIME	METHOD	SERVES
6 Hours 25 minutes	Stove Top / Freezer	8 People

CHEF'S TIPS

- Cornstarch can be used as an alternative to arrowroot to thicken the popsicle.
- Alternatively, try using store bought vegan yogurt instead of the coconut crem and honey mix.

FROZEN
ANNA'S TLT SANDWICHES

INGREDIENTS

- 1 batch/packet of tempeh bacon
- 8 slices of rye bread
- 2 cups of chopped lettuce
- 1 cup sliced cherry tomatoes
- 1 ripe, sliced avocado
- ½ cup of vegan mayonnaise
- 1 tsp crushed garlic

DIRECTIONS

1 Prepare the bacon as per the packet or recipe instructions.

2 Mix the mayo and garlic together in a small bowl.

3 Lightly toast each slice of bread and spread one teaspoon of garlic mayo on each slice.

4 Layer the TLT sandwiches with avocado, cherry tomatoes (sliced in half) lettuce and tempeh bacon.

5 Enjoy!

TIME	METHOD	SERVES
30 minutes	Stove Top	4 Peoples

CHEF'S TIPS

- Drizzle with your favorite chilli sauce before serving.

FROZEN
ELSA'S FROZEN TEA POPSICLES

TIME	METHOD	SERVES
5 Hours 10 minutes	Freezer	8 People

INGREDIENTS

- *2 cups water*
- *2/3 cup organic honey*
- *3/4 cup fresh squeezed lime juice*
- *1/4 cup mint, chopped*

CHEF'S TIPS

Add slices of cucumber and lemon to the popsicle moulds before freezing.

DIRECTIONS

1 Mix the honey in a bowl with water until it dissolves. Add the lime juice.

2 Add the chopped mint and stir until well mixed.

3 Pour the mixture into 8 popsicle molds.

4 Place the popsicles in the freezer for 30 minutes.

5 Remove the popsicles from the freezer and gently add the sticks to the popsicles.

6 Place the popsicles back in the freezer and freeze for a further 4-5 hours.

7 Serve and enjoy!

FROZEN
KRISTOFF'S SWEDISH MEATBALLS

INGREDIENTS

FOR THE MEATBALLS:

- 2 cups water
- ½ chopped red or yellow onion
- 2 tsp minced garlic
- ½ cup of dry brown lentils
- 1 ½ cups chopped mushrooms
- ¾ cup oats
- 2 tsp parsley (dried)
- ¼ tsp allspice
- ¼ tsp nutmeg
- ¼ tsp black pepper
- 2-3 tbsp soy sauce
- 2 tsp vegan Worcestershire sauce

FOR THE GRAVY:

- 1 cup dairy free milk
- 1 can coconut milk
- 1 tbsp soy sauce
- 1 tsp dijon mustard
- 1 tbsp vegan Worcestershire sauce
- 1 tsp garlic powder
- 1 tsp onion powder
- 1 tbsp cornstarch
- 2 T ice cold water.

DIRECTIONS

FOR THE MEATBALLS:

1. Fry the onion in 3 tbsp water in a medium pot until translucent. Add garlic and stir for 2 minutes.
2. Pour in 1.5 cup water and the lentils. Allow the water to boil then lower heat to a simmer for 15-20 minutes. In a separate pot, fry the mushrooms in 3 tbsp water for minutes.
3. Pour oats in a food processor and blend until you have a flour consistency. Add the fried mushrooms, lentils, parsley, allspice, nutmeg, pepper, soy sauce, and
4. Worcestershire sauce to the food processor. Pulse until mixture is combined.
5. Set the mixture aside for 15 minutes.
6. Preheat the oven to 425F degrees Fahrenheit and prepare baking sheet with parchment paper.
7. Roll the mixture from the processor into balls and place on the baking sheet. Bake for 20-25 minutes.

FOR THE GRAVY:

1. Add in all gravy ingredients into a small saucepan, excluding the cornstarch and water.
2. Bring the saucepan to a boil for 2 minutes and then remove from the heat.
3. Whisk the cornstarch and water together in a small mixin bowl until a thick mixture forms. Add this to the gravy..
4. Place the gravy saucepan back on the stove and simmer for 2 minutes.

Serve over the meatballs and enjoy.

TIME	METHOD	MAKES
55 minutes	Stove Top	20 Meatballs

HADE'S STEAMING HOT LEMON RICE SOUP

INGREDIENTS

FOR THE SOUP:

- 2 tbsp cooking oil
- 1 1/2 cups yellow onion, chopped
- 1 cup celery, chopped
- 1 1/2 cups carrot, chopped
- 2 tsp crushed garlic
- 2 vegan stock cubes - vegetable
- 6 cups hot water
- 1 packet dry yeast
- 1 tbsp soy sauce
- 1 cup uncooked rice

FOR THE TAHINI SAUCE:

- 2 tbsp tahini
- 2 tbsp white miso paste
- 1/3 cup lemon juice
- 2 cups stock from soup

DIRECTIONS

1. Add olive oil, onions, carrots, celery and garlic to a large pot on the stove. Cook for 10 minutes on a low heat.

2. Once your veggies are translucent, add stock cubes, water, dry yeast and soy sauce.

3. Bring mixture to a boil and then lower heat before adding the rice.

4. Place a lid on the pot and cook for 20 minutes (or longer) until the rice is fully cooked.

5. Add all the tahini sauce ingredients to a blender and blend until smooth.

6. Once the rice has cooked through, slowly stir in the tahini sauce and stir until mixed through.

7. Serve hot and enjoy!

TIME	METHOD	SERVES
55 minutes	Stove Top	4 People

CHEF'S TIPS

- Add chopped green beans, mini corn or peas to this recipe if you would like to increase the amount of wholesome veggies.

HERCULES' HERCULEAN CHICKPEA GYROS

INGREDIENTS

- 2 tbsp cooking oil
- 1 can chickpeas
- ½ tsp cumin
- ½ tsp oregano
- ¼ tsp paprika
- ¼ tsp garlic powder
- Salt & pepper

ADDITIONAL INGREDIENTS:

- pita breads or naan bread
- Vegan yogurt
- Cucumber - sliced
- Cherry tomatoes - sliced in half
- Red onion - chopped
- Fresh dill
- Spinach

DIRECTIONS

1. Drain the can of chickpeas thoroughly and dab them on a piece of kitchen towel to dry completely.

2. Add the chickpeas to a large pan with oil and season with salt and pepper. Place on medium heat for 8 minutes.

3. Add all the spices and salt and pepper to taste.

4. Stir the chickpeas to coat evenly in all the spices.

5. Allow the mixture to cook for another 2 minutes until the chickpeas are crispy.

6. Scoop the mixture into each pita and layer with the additional ingredients.

TIME	METHOD	MAKES
15 minutes	Stove Top	4 People

HERCULES

INGREDIENTS

FOR THE MEAT BALLS:

- *1 red onion, chopped*
- *2 tsp crushed garlic*
- *5 pitted dates*
- *¼ cup sun-dried tomatoes - sliced*
- *½ cup parsley - fresh*
- *1 tsp fennel seeds*
- *1 tbsp oregano - dried*
- *½ tsp black pepper*
- *¼ cup ground flax seeds*
- *½ cup panko breadcrumbs*
- *½ cup almond flour*
- *1 tsp lemon juice - fresh*
- *2 cans black beans*

FOR THE LEMON DIP:

- *1/3 cup tahini*
- *1 tsp lemon juice - fresh*
- *Paprika*
- *1 tsp crushed garlic*
- *¼ teaspoon black pepper*
- *Water, as needed*

DIRECTIONS

1. Place the first 8 ingredients into a food processor and pulse until finely chopped.

2. Now add the flax seeds, breadcrumbs, almond flour and lemon juice to the food processor and pulse.

3. Add the black beans and process just a few seconds until the beans are slightly mashed.

4. Place this mixture in a bowl and in the fridge for 30 minutes.

5. While the meatball mixture is setting, whisk the tahini with lemon juice, garlic, and black pepper together. Add enough water to make a smooth sauce, according to your desired texture. Add in paprika to taste.

6. Preheat the oven to 375 Fahrenheit.

7. Take the meatball mixture out of the fridge and roll into 20-24 balls using your hands.

8. Place them on a prepared baking sheet and in the middle of the oven. Bake for 50 minutes or until the meatballs start becoming a golden brown color.

9. Serve with the sauce and enjoy!

TIME	METHOD	SERVES
1 Hour 20 minutes	*Oven*	*6 People*

63

MEGARA'S FAVA BEAN SPREAD

INGREDIENTS

- 2 cups fava beans - cooked and peeled
- 1 shallot - chopped
- 2 tsp fresh thyme
- 1 tbsp lemon juice
- 1 tbsp lemon zest
- ½ tsp salt
- ⅓ cup olive oil
- Thyme leaves, lemon zest, fresh ground black pepper to garnish

DIRECTIONS

1. Mix all the ingredients together in a medium bowl— except for the olive oil.

2. Place this mixture in a food processor and pulse until fully combined. Add the olive oil and pulse for 30 seconds.

TIME	METHOD	SERVES
10 minutes	Oven	6 People

CHEF'S TIPS

- Edamame can be used in place of fava beans for a slightly milder taste.
- Spread your Fava bean spread over toast for a light and quick snack.

KRONK'S SPINACH PUFF PINWHEELS

INGREDIENTS

- 1 packet of puff pastry (make sure it is vegan)
- 3 cups of fresh baby spinach
- 2 cups vegan cream cheese
- ½ tsp parsley
- ¼ tsp thyme
- ¼ tsp tarragon
- ½ tsp dill
- 1 tsp onion flakes
- ¾ tsp garlic powder
- Salt to taste
- Sprinkle of allspice

CHEF'S TIPS

- 1 cup thick cashew cream can be used in place of the vegan cream cheese.

DIRECTIONS

1 Boil water and pour it in a bowl. Add spinach and let sit for 2-3 minutes. Drain the spinach using a colander and place it back in the bowl.

2 Add cream cheese and all spices. Stir well and add salt if necessary.

3 Roll it out the packet of puff pastry to a 12 by 14 inch shape. Spoon the cream spinach mixture evenly over the pastry and gently roll the pastry into a long tube.

4 Place the role in the fridge to harden slightly - approximately 1 hour. Refrigerate to harden, about 1 hour.
Remove the spinach roll from the fridge and slice even slices about ¼ - ½ inch thick. You should have approximately 10 pinwheels.

5 On a prepared baking sheet, place each pinwheels lying flat. Bake at 400 deg Fahrenheit for 25 minutes. Your pinwheels should be golden.

6 Serve & enjoy!

TIME	METHOD	MAKES
50 minutes	Oven	10 Pinwheels

YZMA'S BRILLIANT GREEN BREAKFAST SMOOTHIE

INGREDIENTS

- 1 large frozen banana - sliced
- 1/2 ripe avocado
- 1 scoop of vanilla protein powder
- 2 cups of frozen spinach or kale
- 1 cup dairy-free milk

CHEF'S TIPS

- There are many different healthy additions to add to this recipe. You can add your favourite seeds of choice such as sunflower seeds, flax seeds or chia seeds.

DIRECTIONS

1 Add all ingredients to a blender and blend on a high speed.

2 Continue to blend until you have a mixture which is smooth and looks creamy. Depending on your preferences, add dairy free milk to thin out your smoothie or more banana or avocado to thicken.

3 Pour into two glasses and enjoy.

TIME	METHOD	
10 minutes	Blender	2 SERVES

KUZCO'S KOZY SPICED HOT CHOCOLATE

INGREDIENTS

- 2 cups water
- ½ cup cocoa powder - unsweetened
- 2 cinnamon sticks
- 4 allspice balls
- 1 cup dairy free milk
- 1 can vegan condensed milk

DIRECTIONS

1 Boil the 2 cups of water on the stove.

2 Slowly stir in the cocoa powder and add in the cinnamon sticks and allspice balls.

3 Reduce the heat and simmer for 5 minutes, stirring continuously.

4 Slowly add the milk and stir in ½ of the condensed milk.
Taste the mixture and add more condensed milk if you would like it sweeter.

5 Let the mixture simmer for 2 more minutes and then serve.

TIME	METHOD	SERVES
10 minutes	Stove Top	2 People

CHEF'S TIPS

- If you do not have vegan condensed milk, you can make your own with two ingredients. You will need 1 can of full fat coconut milk and ⅓ cup of brown, organic sugar. Mix them together and simmer on a low heat for 45 minutes. Voila!

CHICHA AND PACHA'S SWEET POTATO MASH

INGREDIENTS

- 8 cups sweet potato - cut into small cubes
- 6 tbsp vegan butter
- 2 tsp crushed garlic
- 2 tbsp dry yeast
- 1 tsp dill
- ½ tsp nutmeg
- ½ tsp salt
- ground black pepper, to taste

DIRECTIONS

1 Fill a large pot with water and add half a teaspoon of sal Bring the water to a boil, and then add in your diced swe potatos. Cook until they become tender, this will take about ten minutes.

2 Drain the potatoes and add them back to the pot.

3 Add the remaining ingredients (except the pecans) and mash with a potato masher until smooth. Top with pecans and serve immediately!

CHEF'S TIPS

- Sprinkle ⅓ cup pecan nuts on top of the mash before serving.

TIME	METHOD	SERVES
25 minutes	Stove Top	6 People

A BUG'S LIFE
FLIK'S DIRT CAKE

INGREDIENTS

FOR THE CAKE:

- 1 ½ cup all-purpose flour
- 3 scoops protein powder - vanilla/chocolate flavor
- ¾ cup cocoa powder
- ½ cup granulated sugar
- 1 tbsp baking powder
- 1 cup dairy free milk (any kind)
- ½ cup apple sauce
- 2 flax eggs
- 1 tsp vanilla essence
- ½ cup vegan butter
- 2 tbsp Dark Chocolate Chips - dairy free

FOR THE FROSTING:

- 16 oz vegan cream cheese
- 1 cup icing sugar
- 12 Chocolate Sandwich Cookies

(One vegan brand is Newman's Own Newman O's)

Oreos can have cross contact with milk ingredients, this is why we don't recommend it.

DIRECTIONS

1. Preheat the oven to 350 degrees Fahrenheit.
2. Prepare 2 x 8 inch round cake pans by spraying with nonstick cooking spray.
3. In a large mixing bowl, add all the dry ingredients and stir together until well combined.
4. Add the flax eggs and milk to a bowl and whisk together before adding the vanilla essence and apple sauce.
5. Place the chocolate chips in a small bowl and soften in the microwave for 50 seconds. Add the vegan butter and mix together until you have a smooth and creamy mixture.
6. Slowly add the egg mixture to the dry ingredients and stir until well mixed. Add the chocolate mixture and continue to stir until you have a smooth cake mixture.
7. Pour the cake batter to the two cake pans.
8. Place in the oven for 30 minutes or until a toothpick comes out clean when pierced through the middle of the cake. Remove from the oven and set aside to cool.

FOR THE FROSTING AND CHOCOLATE COOKIE COATING:

1. Stir the vegan cream cheese and icing sugar together. Finely crush the Oreos in a blender or food processor.
2. Spread a thick layer of the cream cheese mixture over the top of one of the cake layers before placing the second layer on top.
3. Coat the outside of two layers with the crea, cheese mixture and sprinkle the crushed oreo over the top and sides of the cake.

TIME	METHOD	SERVES
40 minutes	Oven	12 People

HOPPER'S ANTS ON A LOG

INGREDIENTS

- 6 sticks of celery
- 6 tbsp peanut butter (sugar free)
- ¼ cup raisins

CHEF'S TIPS

- Tip: If your raisins are a bit dry or hard, you can microwave them for a few seconds or soak them in warm water for a minute to plump up. Dry well before adding to peanut butter.

DIRECTIONS

1. Wash the celery. Remove any dried ends and chop off the leafy green part of the celery so you are left with the stalks. Rinse these stalks thoroughly and dab dry with a clean cloth.

2. Cut each celery stick in half.

3. Using a butter knife, spread peanut butter down the middle of each celery stick.

4. Sprinkle the raisins on top.

5. Serve and enjoy!

TIME	MAKES
10 minutes	12 Sticks

PRINCESS ATTA'S CHIA SEED PUDDING

INGREDIENTS

- 1 cup of dairy free milk
- ½ tsp orange zest
- ⅛ tsp vanilla essence
- 3 tablespoons chia seeds
- Topping ideas: maple syrup, sliced bananas, blueberries, raspberries, coconut flakes and raw nuts

CHEF'S TIPS

If you don't have time to let the pudding set overnight, you could place it in the fridge for 2 hours. This is the minimum amount of time needed for the pudding to set.

DIRECTIONS

1. Stir the milk, orange zest and vanilla essence together in a bowl , cup or glass jar.

2. Add the chia seeds and whisk the mixture briskly. Set the mixture aside for 15 minutes.

3. Whisk the mixture again to ensure there are no clumps and the chia seeds are completely mixed in.

4. Cover the bowl and place in the fridge overnight.

5. Stir the mixture once more before serving. Drizzle over some maple syrup and add any of your favorite toppings.

6. Serve and enjoy!

TIME	METHOD	MAKES
2 Hours 5 Minutes	Refrigerator	1 Large Pudding

DOT'S POLKADOT CHOCOLATE BARK

INGREDIENTS

- 2 cups chocolate chips (70% cacao is 100% vegan as it contains no dairy)

OR

- Coconut Milk Chocolate Chips
- ¼ cup white chocolate chips (vegan)
- ¼ cup raisins
- 3 tbsp raw or roasted cashews
- 3 tbsp chopped almonds
- ¼ cup dried cranberries
- 3 tbsp pumpkin seeds
- 3 tbsp chopped pecans

CHEF'S TIPS

- These delicious chocolate bark pieces can be stored in the fridge and enjoyed for up to a week.

DIRECTIONS

1. Prepare 2 x 9-inch square baking pans by lining them wi baking paper and spraying them with non-stick spray.

2. Using a double boiler, melt the dark chocolate chips ov low heat while stirring continuously.

3. Pour half of the melted chocolate into each of the pans and ensure that the mixture is evenly spread between across the pan. The best way to do this is to tilt each pa and allow the mixture to spread.

4. Sprinkle the white chocolate chips over the chocolate mixture and gently press them slightly into the dark chocolate so that they are slightly embedded.

5. Sprinkle the cashews, chopped almonds, pumpkin seeds, pecans, cranberries, and raisins in between the white chocolate chips, ensuring they are evenly spread out.

6. Place each pan in the fridge for 1 hour to allow the chocolate to set.

7. Peel the baking paper off from the baking pan and place the chocolate on a chopping board.

8. Use your hands to break the chocolate into rough pieces which resemble bark.

TIME	METHOD	SERVES
1 Hour 30 Minutes	Stove Top	12 People

THE LION KING
NALA'S PEANUT SWEET POTATO SOUP

TIME	METHOD	SERVES
45 minutes	*Stove Top*	*4-6 People*

INGREDIENTS

- 4 tsp of crushed garlic (ideally fresh)
- 3 tsp of crushed ginger (ideally fresh)
- 1 tspb of fresh cilantro, chopped
- 1 jalapeño chili, chopped and stem removed
- Salt
- 2 cans full-fat coconut milk (or coconut cream)
- 2 tbsp cooking oil
- 6 scallions, chopped
- 1 tsp ground turmeric
- 4 cups of vegetable stock
- 1 cup sweet potato, peeled and diced
- 2 cups unsalted peanuts
- 2 tsps sugar
- 5 oz fresh kale, roughly chopped & stems removed
- 1 tbsp lime juice, fresh
- Black pepper, freshly ground
- 3 cups Jasmine rice

DIRECTIONS

1 *Using a mortar and pestle, grind the garlic, ginger, cilantro and half the ginger into a paste. Add a sprinkle of salt and set aside.*

2 *Place a large saucepan on medium heat and add 3 spoonfuls of fat from the top of the coconut milk can and 1 tablespoon of cooking oil. Stir frequently.*

3 *Continue stirring until the coconut milk turns a light golden brown. Add the paste from the mortar and pestle and continue to stir. Add half of the scallions and turmeric and continue to cook for approximately 1 minute.*

4 *Pour in the remaining coconut milk from both cans as well as 1 quart of vegetable stock.*

5 *Add in the sweet potatoes and turn up the heat of the pan to bring to a boil.*

6 *Reduce the pan to a simmer and cook until sweet potatoes are cooked through.*

7 *Using a small pan, combine peanuts and remaining cooking oil and place on medium heat. Stir the peanuts and allow to cook until they are a dark golden brown. Remove from the heat and set aside.*

8 *Roughly chop half of the peanuts and place the other half into the mortar and pestle. Add 1 teaspoon of sugar and a pinch of salt and grind the peanuts to create a rough paste. Add this paste to the sweet potato saucepan and repeat with the remaining peanuts.*

9 *Using a hand blender directly in the pot, blend the sweet potato mixture.*

10 *Allow the mixture to simmer again and stir in the kale until it has wilted, followed by the lime juice. Stir in lime juice.*

11 *Stir in cilantro and serve soup with rice and garnish with remaining sliced chilies.*

TIMON AND PUMBA'S MISR WAT

INGREDIENTS

- 1 ½ tbsp coconut oil or vegan butter
- ¾ tbsp mild curry spice
- 1 tsp crushed garlic
- ¼ tbsp crushed ginger
- ½ tsp cumin
- ½ tsp dried coriander
- ½ tsp smoked paprika
- ½ tbsp tomato puree
- 1 ½ cups vegetable stock
- ½ cup brown lentils (from a can)
- ½ head cauliflower
- ½ onion finely chopped
- ½ cup peas (fresh or frozen)

CHEF'S TIPS

- Add water to the pan when cooking the onions and lentils to prevent sticking to the pan.

DIRECTIONS

1 Place coconut oil in a large saucepan on a medium heat. . . Once the oil has melted, add the onion, garlic, ginger and curry spice.

2 Cook and stir until the onions become translucent.

3 Add your lentils (which you have drained), cauliflower (chopped) and tomato puree, stirring for around 3 minutes until well combined.

4 Stir in the vegetable stock and increase heat of the pan to bring to a boil.

5 Once boiling, reduce heat and allow mixture to simmer for approximately 30 minutes.

6 Add salt and pepper to taste.

7 Top with a generous dollop of vegan sour cream (optional)

TIME	METHOD	SERVES
30 minutes	Stove Top	4 People

THE LION KING
SCAR'S CALLALOO SOUP

INGREDIENTS

- 8 cups baby spinach
- 1 ½ cups sweet potato, diced
- 1 ½ cups butternut or pumpkin, diced
- 1 cup red onion, diced
- 2 tsp crushed garlic
- ½ tbsp thyme, dried
- ¼ habanero chili, diced
- 1 tsp of himalayan salt
- 1 large scallion, chopped
- ¼ tsp black pepper
- 1 tbsp cornstarch
- 2 cups vegetable stock
- 2 cups coconut milk
- 2 tbsp coconut oil

CHEF'S TIPS

- The Habanero chilli can be replaced with a scotch bonnet which adds a slightly sweeter taste.

DIRECTIONS

1 Heat the coconut oil in a large saucepan over medium heat.

2 For the onion, scallion and crushed garlic until the onions are translucent and soft.

3 Add the butternut, sweet potato and scallions to the sautéed onions and garlic.

4 Allow all of the vegetables to cook for 3 to 5 minutes, stirring continuously so that they don't burn.

5 Add the habanero chilli , thyme, salt and pepper.

6 Add the baby spinach into the pan, and stir to allow the spinach to wilt.

7 Stir in the coconut milk, the cornstarch and the vegetable stock.

8 Reduce the heat, place a lid on the saucepan and allow the mixture to simmer. This will allow the mixture to thicken and will take approximately an hour.

9 Once the soup reaches your desired thickness, use a hand blender to liquidise the last of the vegetables. Serve hot and enjoy.

TIME	METHOD	SERVES
1 Hour 20 Minutes	Stove Top	4-6 People

THE LION KING
SIMBA'S BLACK EYED PEA FRITTERS

INGREDIENTS

- ¾ cup black-eyed peas, cooked or soaked overnight
- ½ red onion, chopped
- 1 small jalapeno chilli, chopped
- 1 tsp crushed ginger
- 2 bay leaves
- Salt, to taste
- Cooking oil

CHEF'S TIPS

- You can use any variant of your favorite bean in this dish! Yum!

DIRECTIONS

1. Remove the skin of each of the black-eyed peas by rubbing them between your fingers.

2. Place the insides of the beans into a mortar and pestle and grind into a paste. If it comes very thick, add a few drops of water.

3. Place a small saucepan on the stove and add enough cooking oil to deep fry.

4. Add the onion, jalapenos, chilli, ginger, bay leaves and salt to the bean paste. This is now the batter to be deep fried.

5. Add a spoonful of batter to the hot oil one at a time and allow to become golden brown.

6. Remove from the oil once crispy and brown and drain or paper towels.

7. Serve hot and enjoy!.

TIME	METHOD	SERVES
3 Hours	Stove Top	4 People

ZAZU'S COCONUT AND TURMERIC POTATOES

INGREDIENTS

- 2 large potatoes cut into wedges
- 2 tbsp coconut flour
- 1 tsp ground turmeric
- 3 tbsp coconut oil
- 1 Vegetable stock cube

CHEF'S TIPS

- *This dish can be served on its own with your favorite sauce or as a side dish to complement any main.*

DIRECTIONS

1 Place a medium sized pot on the stove and fill it halfway with water.

2 Add the potatoes and allow the water to boil.
Once boiling, reduce the heat and allow it to simmer for a few minutes.

3 Drain the potatoes using a colander.

4 For the potato coating. Add the flour, turmeric, oil and stock cube to a small mixing bowl and stir until you have a smooth paste.

5 Cover the potatoes in the paste and spread them evenly in an oven pan lined with baking paper.

6 Drizzle the potatoes with coil and cover the pan with aluminium foil.

7 Prick a few small holes in the foil to allow the hot air to escape.

8 Place in the oven for 40 minutes. Remove the foil halfway.

TIME	METHOD	SERVES
60 minutes	*Stove Top / Oven*	*2 People*

THE LION KING
MUFASA'S JOLLOF RICE

TIME	METHOD	SERVES
60 minutes	*Stove Top / Oven*	*2 People*

INGREDIENTS

- 2 tbsp cooking oil
- ½ large onion, diced
- 2 tsp crushed garlic
- 1 tsp of crushed ginger
- 4 Thai chili peppers, thinly sliced
- 1 tsp salt
- 1 cup uncooked rice (jasmine or basmati)
- ½ tsp paprika
- 1 tsp dried thyme
- 1 can chopped tomatoes
- 1 cup vegetable stock
- Fresh parsley for serving

DIRECTIONS

1 *Over medium heat, place the cooking oil in a large saucepan. Add the onions and fry until they become translucent.*

2 *Stir in the crushed garlic, ginger and chilis. Continue to stir and cook until the spices give off their fragrance.*

3 *Stir in the rice and salt and allow some time for the rice to brown. Now add the paprika, thyme, crushed tomatoes and vegetable stock. Give the mixture a good stir.*

4 *Reduce the heat of the plate to low and place a lid on the pan. Allow the pan to simmer until all the stock is absorbed. Stir occasionally. This takes approximately 15 minutes.*

5 *Remove the pan from the stove and allow the rice to rest for 10 minutes. Mix the mix using a fork before serving.*

6 *Enjoy!*

CHEF'S TIPS

Serve with slices of fried plaintain on the side.

ATLANTIS: THE LOST EMPIRE
PRINCESS KITA'S "CRAB" CAKES

TIME	METHOD	SERVES
30 minutes	*Stove Top*	*6 People*

INGREDIENTS

- *1 can chickpeas, drained*
- *1 can asparagus, chopped*
- *1 can artichoke heart, drained*
- *1 ½ cups breadcrumbs*
- *¾ cup mayonnaise (vegan)*
- *1 tsp dijon mustard*
- *2 tsp lemon juice*
- *¼ tsp salt and ¼ tsp pepper*
- *1 tsp allspice*
- *1 tbsp cooking oil*
- *1 tbsp pickle relish*

CHEF'S TIP:

Add corn to this fish cake mix for an extra bit of texture and sweet taste.

DIRECTIONS

1. Add chickpeas, asparagus, and artichoke hearts to a blender or food processor. Pulse until mixture is just chopped.

2. Place this mixture into a mixing bowl and add 1 cup of the bread crumbs, ¼ cup mayonnaise, the mustard, 1 tsp lemon juice, salt, pepper and the all spice mix.

3. Stir the mixture until well combined and then make 6 x 1 inch patties using your hands and roll each patty in the remaining breadcrumbs.

4. Place a frying pan on the stove on a high heat and add the cooking oil.

5. Fry each patty on both sides for approximately 4 minutes on each side.

6. Remove them from the pan and allow them to cool off on a piece of paper towel to absorb any excess oil.

7. To make a dip for your crab cakes, mix the remaining mayo, relish and 1 teaspoon lemon juice together.

8. Serve and enjoy!

ATLANTIS: THE LOST EMPIRE
ATLANTEAN SEAWEED SALAD

INGREDIENTS

- 1 oz dried seaweed (wakame)
- 3 tbsp rice vinegar
- 3 tbsp tamari sauce
- 1 tbsp sesame oil
- 1 Tsp crushed garlic
- 3 green onions, sliced
- 1 green apple - sliced into strips
- 2 tbsp cilantro, chopped
- 1 tbsp white sesame seeds
- ¼ tsp red chilli flakes

DIRECTIONS

1 Place seaweed in a bowl of warm water and soak for 5 minutes. Drain the seaweed and squeeze out all excess water.

2 Slice the seaweed into ½ inch pieces.

3 Combine the rice vinegar, tamari sauce, sesame oil, crushed ginger, crushed garlic, onions, cilantro, sesame seeds and red pepper flakes. Mix until well combined.

4 In a separate mixing bowl, stir the seaweed, apple and cilantro together.

5 Add the rice vinegar mixture and stir. Top with sesame seeds.

6 Serve and enjoy!

CHEF'S TIPS

- *Serve as a side dish or a healthy meal on its own.*

TIME	MAKES
15 minutes	4 People

COOKIE'S WHITE BEAN MASH

INGREDIENTS

- *1 can butter beans*
- *2 sprigs rosemary*
- *2 tsp crushed garlic*
- *2 spring onions, chopped*
- *¼ tsp salt*
- *¼ tsp black pepper*
- *1 tsp tomato puree*
- *2 olive oil*

CHEF'S TIPS

- *This dish can be served heated or be served cold.*

DIRECTIONS

1. Remove the beans from the can and rinse them under water.

2. Place a saucepan on medium heat on the stove and add olive oil.

3. Add the crushed garlic, 1 sprig of rosemary and tomato purée to the pan. Stir.

4. Add the rinsed beans to the pan and stir for about 5 minutes. Add the salt and pepper.

5. Remove the sprig of rosemary.

6. Remove the plan from the heat and add the ingredients to a food processor or blender.

7. Stir in the chopped spring onions and place mash into a serving bowl.

8. Place the 2nd sprig of rosemary on the top to garnish and serve!

TIME	METHOD	SERVES
15 minutes	*Stove Top*	*2-4 People*

ARIEL'S SWEET POTATO SUSHI

TIME	METHOD	SERVES
45 minutes	*Oven*	*1-2 People*

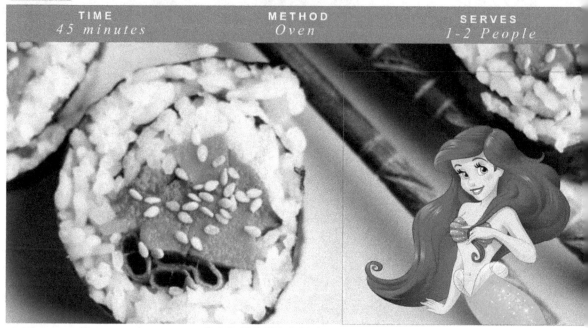

INGREDIENTS

FOR THE SUSHI FILLING (SWEET POTATO):

- *1 tbsp olive oil*
- *1 tbsp maple syrup*
- *1 tsp sesame oil*
- *1 large sweet potato, peeled and cut into strips*

FOR THE RICE:

- *1 cup sushi rice*
- *1 ⅓ cups water*
- *1 ½ tbsp rice vinegar*
- *¾ tbsp salt*

FOR THE ROLLING AND SERVING:

- *3 sheets nori*

DIRECTIONS

1 Preheat the oven to 375° Fahrenheit. Prepare a baking tray by lining with baking paper and spraying with non-stick spray.

2 Add the olive oil, maple syrup and sesame oil together in a small bowl.

3 Toss the strips of sweet potato into the oil oil mixture and place on the baking tray.

4 Bake for 25 minutes, turning the pieces half way through. In the interim, rinse the sushi rice under cold running water for 1 minute.

5 Place a small saucepan on the stove with the water, vinegar and salt. Add the rice and bring to a boil. Reduce the heat immediately and allow it to simmer. Place a lid on the saucepan and simmer for 15 minutes or until all the water is absorbed.

6 Remove rice from the stove and set aside.

7 Fill a small container with water to wet your hands. Roll out the bamboo mat and place one of the nori sheets on the bamboo mat.

8 Using your hands, create a thin layer of rice over the nori. Place ⅓ of the sweet potato strips in a single line along the width of nori.

9 Starting with one end of the bamboo mat, roll the mat tightly over the fillings. Tuck the sheet or nori underneath to that the filling is completely enclosed. Use the bamboo mat to compress and tighten the roll.

10 Once your sweet potato sushi is tightly rolled, slice into even pieces. You should get approximately 6 - 8 pieces. Serve with soy sauce, pickled ginger and wasabi.

THE LITTLE MERMAID
SEBASTIAN'S "CLAM" CHOWDER

TIME	METHOD	MAKES
30 minutes	*Oven*	*15 Cookies*

INGREDIENTS

FOR THE CREAM BASE

- ½ cup raw cashews, soaked in warm water for an hour
- ¾ cup unsweetened dairy free milk
- For the mushrooms
- 1 tbsp coconut oil
- 8 oz button mushrooms, cut in half
- 1 tsp crushed garlic
- 1 tsp tamari sauce

FOR THE SOUP BASE

- 2 tbsp coconut oil
- 1 yellow onion, chopped
- 2 celery stalks, chopped
- 3 medium carrots, sliced
- 2 tsp crushed garlic
- 1 tsp thyme (dried)
- ½ cup white wine (vegan)
- 4 cups vegetable stock
- 3 tablespoons all-purpose flour
- 2 medium potatoes, diced
- 2 bay leaves
- 2 tsp dried seaweed
- ½ tsp salt
- 1 tbsp fresh lemon juice
- Black pepper to taste

DIRECTIONS

1 Blend the dairy free milk & cashews in a blender or food processor until smooth and set aside.

2 Add the coconut oil in a large saucepan over high heat. Add the mushrooms and saute until mushrooms start to brown.

3 Add the minced garlic and soy sauce. Remove the mushrooms from the pan and set aside.

4 Using the same pot, heat the coconut oil over medium heat. Add onion and fry until the onions become translucent.

5 Stir in the celery, carrots, garlic and dried thyme. Continue to stir and fry the veggies until they start to become tender.

6 Pour in the wine and bring the pot to a simmer. Once the pot starts to simmer reduce the heat again and allow the wine time to reduce while stirring often.

7 Sprinkle the all-purpose flour over the wine and continue to stir. Slowly pour in the vegetable stock followed by the potatoes, bay leaf, seaweed and salt to taste.

8 Bring the pot to a simmer and allow to cook until the potatoes are tender. Reduce the pot to a low heat. Slowly pour in cashew cream and stir in until completely combined.

10 Garnish with parsley, serve and enjoy!

THE LITTLE MERMAID
KING TRITON'S KING OYSTER POPCORN SHRIMP

TIME	METHOD	SERVES
60 minutes	*Deep Fryer*	*4 People*

CHEF'S TIP:
Serve with lemon wedges to be squeezed over the shrimp before eating.

NGREDIENTS

FOR THE "SHRIMP":

- *4 large oyster mushroom stems, sliced into thick pieces.*
- *For the "crumbs"*
- *½ cup coconut flour*
- *1 ½ cup dairy free milk*
- *1 tsp apple cider vinegar*
- *1 tbsp ground flax seeds*
- *3 tbsp water*
- *¾ cup all-purpose flour*
- *¼ cup cornstarch*
- *1 tbsp garlic powder*
- *1 tbsp onion powder*
- *2 cups breadcrumbs*
- *Vegetable oil for frying*

FOR THE DIP:

- *1 cup mayonnaise*
- *½ cup sweet chili sauce*
- *2 tbsp sriracha sauce*
- *1 tsp lime juice*

DIRECTIONS

1 Cut each scallop into 2 shrimp-like shapes. They don't need to be perfect.

2 Add the coconut flour to one bowl.

3 In a separate mixing bowl, whisk together the dairy free milk, vinegar and flax egg. (Make the flax egg with 1 tbsp flaxseeds to 3 tbsp water)

4 Mix the all-purpose flour, cornstarch, garlic and onion powder together. Slowly mix this together with the milk mixture.

5 In a third bowl, add the breadcrumbs.

6 Mix all of the ingredients for the bang bang sauce together and set aside for until the shrimp is ready to serve.

7 Place a deep fryer or cast iron pot to the stove on high heat and pour in several inches of oil.

8 You are now ready to assemble and cook the "shrimp". Place a mushroom in the coconut flour, dunk it into the batter and then coat it in the bread crumbs.

9 Cook the mushroom in the hot oil and allow it to fry until it is golden brown.

10 Serve hot with a side of your dip.

FLOUNDER'S MUSHROOM CALAMARI

INGREDIENTS

- 4 – 5 Large King Oyster Mushrooms
- 1 half a lemon, cut into wedges (for garnish)
- Vegan tartar sauce (or shrimp cocktail sauce if preferred)
- Oil for frying (vegetable, safflower oil or peanut oil all work fine)

CHEF'S TIPS

- To really take your calamari to the next level, add these extras: lemon wedges, chopped parsley, coconut vinegar.

TIME
30 minutes

METHOD
Stove Top

SERVES
4 People

DIRECTIONS

1. Cut off the mushroom caps, and store them for another use. Take the king oyster stems, and slice them into rounds that are about 1/8th to 1/4th inches in thickness.

2. Using either a cookie cutter, a sharp knife, or an icing piping tip, carefully cut / punch a hole into the centre of each round to create a ring. Do not discard the centres of the rings, they will fried up as well. Put them in a bowl.

3. For the batter, mix the flour, cayenne pepper, paprika, cornstarch, garlic powder, ground pepper and sea salt into a medium sized bowl. Pour the club soda into the bowl slowly, and keep whisking. You should end up with a batter that is the same consistency as pancake batter.

4. Whether you use a pot or a deep fryer, is up to you. If using a pot, make sure it is flat bottomed and pour about 2 inches of vegetable oil into it. Now heat up your oil to 350°F. Once this temperature is reached, your mushrooms are ready for frying!

5. Add half of your mushroom calamari pieces into the batter and make sure they are evenly coated. Let the excess batter drip off, before gently adding them into the frying oil, a couple pieces at a time. (If you find them starting to stick together, use a wooden chopstick, or spoon to poke them away from one another).

6. Cook for about two minute, and as they begin to float to the top of the oil, flip them over and cook for an additional two minutes. When they are a nice golden brown all over, they are ready!

7. Line a baking sheet with paper towel to move your calamari onto. Use a slotted spoon to take the cooked mushrooms out of the fryer or pot. Repeat the above steps, battering and frying all of your remaining mushroom rings and pieces, until they are all cooked.

8. Serve hot with a side of lemon wedges to squeeze over your calamari, and with your favorite vegan tartar sauce. (Or try it with shrimp cocktail sauce!)

URSULA FAUX FISH BURGER

INGREDIENTS

FOR THE FISH FILLETS:

1 block firm tofu

½ cup breadcrumbs

1 tsp lemon zest

¼ tsp dill (dried)

¼ tsp curry powder

¼ tsp paprika powder

¼ tsp salt

½ sheet nori seaweed

2 tbsp all-purpose flour

2 tbsp water

½ tsp salt

Cooking oil

Burger buns

**FOR THE GARLIC
YOGHURT SAUCE:**

½ cup vegan yogurt

1 tsp dill

1 tsp crushed garlic

Salt to taste

DIRECTIONS

1 Remove the tofu from its packaging and wrap it in a paper towel with a heavier object on top to press all the liquid out of the tofu.

2 Combine the flour with 2 tablespoons of water and add ½ teaspoon of salt. This will make an 'egg' replacement dip for your tofu.

3 Prepare the coating of the fish by mixing the breadcrumbs, lemon zest, dill, curry powder, paprika powder, salt and dried seaweed.

4 Slice the tofu into 4 even pieces and dip them in the egg replacement (flour + water + salt), followed by the breadcrumbs.

5 Fry the tofu in a hot pan with olive oil until they are golden on each side. Repeat for all the slices and pan-fry them in a large pan with olive oil until they're crispy and golden on both sides.

6 Assemble your burger with your favorite burger toppings.

7 For the garlic yogurt sauce, stir all the ingredients together and spread over your burger bun.

TIME	METHOD	SERVES
1 Hour 20 minutes	*Stove Top*	*4 People*

PETER PAN'S BLACK BEAN BURGERS

INGREDIENTS

- 8 ounces button mushrooms
- 1 medium carrot
- 1 ½ cups broccoli florets
- ½ small onion
- 2 tsp crushed garlic
- 2 tbsp olive oil
- 1 tsp smoked paprika
- 1 tsp chili powder
- ¾ tsp salt
- ½ tsp black pepper
- 1 can black beans
- ⅓ cup walnuts, chopped
- 3 cups baby spinach leaves
- ½ cup breadcrumbs
- 2 flax eggs
- 1 tbsp tomato paste
- ¾ cup cooked brown rice
- Bread rolls and you hamburger favorite toppings

CHEF'S TIPS

- Mix 1 tbsp ground flaxseed with 3 tbsp of water to make one egg

DIRECTIONS

1. Preheat the oven to 400 degrees Fahrenheit. Prepare two baking trays by lining them with baking paper and non-stick spray.
2. Chop the mushrooms, carrot, broccoli and onion into chunks and place them in a food processor. Before pulsing, add the garlic, olive oil, smoked paprika, chili powder, salt and pepper. Pulse until the mixture is coarsely ground.
3. Spread a layer of this vegetable mix onto one of the baking sheets and roast for 15 minutes.
4. While the vegetables are roasting, spread the black beans over the second baking tray.
5. Meanwhile, spread the drained black beans onto the second baking sheet in one layer and place in the oven until the sides of the beans start to split.
6. Remove both trays from the oven and allow to cool.
7. Add the walnuts, spinach and herbs to a food processor. Pulse until you have a coarse mixture.
8. Add the beans and pulse until the beans are evenly mixed in.
9. Now add the roasted vegetables, breadcrumbs, eggs and tomato paste. Pulse once more until evenly mixed through.
10. Use your hands to create evenly sized burger patties. Fry in a heated oil on each side for 3 minutes.
11. Assemble the burgers with your favorite toppings and burger buns. Enjoy!

TIME	METHOD	SERVES
45 minutes	Oven	6 People

PETER PAN
THE LOST BOYS TRAIL MIX

INGREDIENTS

- 2 cups mixed nuts
- 1 cup mixed seeds sunflower seeds, pumpkin seeds etc.
- ¼ cup dried cranberries,
- ¼ cup of raisins
- ¼ cup dried mango
- 2 tbsp dark chocolate chips (vegan)

CHEF'S TIPS

- Be creative with this recipe and replace any of the nuts or dried fruits with your favorites.

DIRECTIONS

1 Roast the nuts in the oven at 350 degrees Fahrenheit for 10 - 15 minutes. You can skip this step if you prefer raw nuts.

2 Chop all dried fruit into smaller, snack size pieces.

3 Mix the nuts, dried fruit and chocolate together and place in an airtight container.

4 Enjoy your homemade and healthy trail mix.

TIME	SERVES
5 minutes	2 People

PETER PAN
CAPTAIN HOOK'S HASH BROWN SAND DOLLARS

TIME	METHOD	SERVES
50 minutes	*Oven*	*4 People*

CHEF'S TIP:
These Sand Dollar stacks can be frozen and stored for up to 4 weeks.

INGREDIENTS

- 4 cups finely grated potatoes
- 1 shallot, sliced
- ¼ cup fresh parsley
- ½ cup cooked corn
- 2 tbsp melted vegan butter
- 1 tbsp cornstarch
- ½ tsp sea salt
- ½ tsp black pepper

DIRECTIONS

1 Preheat the oven to 375 degrees Fahrenheit.

2 Spray a standard size muffin tin with non-stick spray.

3 Place grated potatoes in a mixing bowl with all other ingredients and mix until well combined.

4 Divide the mixture between the 12 muffin moulds.

5 Place in the oven and bake for 40 minutes.

6 Remove from the oven and allow to cool slightly before using a butter knife to loosen each hash brown.

7 Serve hot!

PETER PAN
TINKERBELL'S COCONUT CHEESECAKE BROWNIE BITES

TIME	METHOD	SERVES
1 Hour 5 Minutes	Oven	4 People

CHEF'S TIP:
Add rum extract to the brownie batter or cheesecake batter if you have some.

NGREDIENTS

DIRECTIONS

FOR THE BROWNIE:

- *½ cup oat flour*
- *¼ cup coconut flour*
- *2 tbsp cocoa powder*
- *¼ tsp baking powder*
- *1 tbsp flax meal*
- *2 tbsp dairy-free milk*
- *¼ cup maple syrup*
- *¼ cup vegan chocolate chips*
- *1 tsp vanilla essence*
- *1/8 tsp salt*
- *2 tbsp vegetable oil*
- *¼ cup ground raw sugar*
- *¼ cup of choc chips (vegan)*

FOR THE CHEESECAKE:

- *8 oz firm tofu*
- *2 tbsp coconut flour*
- *2 tbsp vegetable oil*
- *3 tbsp raw sugar*
- *1 tsp vanilla essence*
- *1 tsp lemon juice*
- *⅓ tsp salt*

FOR THE BROWNIE:

1 Mix all the dry brownie ingredients together in a medium mixing bowl.
Heat the milk and maple syrup until hot by combining them and placing them in the microwave.

2 Stir in the flaxseed meal and dark chocolate until melted.
Slowly add in the wet ingredients into the dry and stir until well combined.

3 Add the vegan chocolate chips into the batter and pour the batter into a prepared baking pan.

FOR THE CHEESECAKE:

4 Preheat the oven to 250 degrees Fahrenheit

5 Drain all excess liquid from the tofu and add it to a blender along with remaining cheesecake ingredients. Add lemon juice if desired to teak the cream cheese desired taste.

6 Pour over the brownie layer and spread evenly and place in the oven for 40 minutes.

7 Once cooked, place in the oven for 30 minutes before serving.

POCAHONTAS
POCAHONTAS'S "THREE SISTERS" VEGETABLE STEW

INGREDIENTS

- 1 large butternut squash , cut in half and seeds removed
- 2 tbsp cooking oil
- 1 onion, chopped
- 2 tsp crushed garlic
- 1 medium green pepper, cut into slices
- 1 can roasted diced tomatoes
- 1 can pinto beans, drained and rinsed
- 2 cups corn kernels
- 1 cup vegetable stock
- 2 small fresh hot chilis - seeds removed and finely chopped
- 2 tsp ground cumin
- 2 tsp chili powder
- 1 tsp dried oregano
- Salt and freshly ground black pepper
- ¼ cup fresh parsley
- **OPTIONAL:** Vegan Bacon (chopped into small pieces)

DIRECTIONS

1 Preheat the oven to 375 degrees Fahrenheit.

2 Place the two butternut halves face up on a prepared baking tray and cover with tin foil.

3 Bake for 40 - 50 minutes. To test if cooked, you should be able to piece through the skin of the butternut easily with a sharp knife.

4 Once cooked, allow the butternut to cool until it is at a temperature you can handle with your hands.

5 Cut each half into small cubes.

6 Place your soup pot on medium heat and add cooking oil. Add the onion and fry until they become translucent.

7 Stir in the crushed garlic and continue to fry until the onion becomes golden.

8 Add the butternut to the soup pot as well as the remaining soup ingredients besides the parsley and salt and pepper.

9 Bring the pot to a boil and then reduce to a simmer. Cover the pot and allow it to simmer until all the vegetables become tender. This should take approximately 20 minutes. Add the salt and pepper to taste. Stir in the parsley and serve!

TIME	METHOD	SERVES
1 Hour 40 Minutes	Oven	10 People

KOCOUM'S BUTTERNUT SQUASH SOUP

INGREDIENTS

- 1 cup carrots, chopped
- 1 cup celery, chopped
- 1 bay leaf
- 6 sprigs parsley
- 4 sprigs thyme
- 1 tbsp peppercorns, whole
- 1 cup dry white wine
- 5 cups water
- 1 ½ cups onions, diced
- 3 cups butternut, diced
- Salt and black pepper, to taste
- Pinch of nutmeg

OPTIONAL:

- 1 apple

CHEF'S TIPS

- For an extra touch of sweetness, peel, core and chop up an apple and add it into the boiling pot with the rest of the veggies.

DIRECTIONS

1 Place a large pot on medium heat with some cooking oil.

2 Add the carrots, celery, parsley, thyme, peppercorns, bay leaf, white wine, water, and onions (keep ¼ of the onion aside).

3 Bring the pot to a boil and then reduce to a simmer. Allow the pot to simmer for 2 to 3 hours.

4 Strain the contents of the pot through a sieve and return to the pot. Discard the contents in the sieve.

5 Add the butternut and ¼ portion of onion to the pot. Allow to cook until the butternut is tender.

6 Using a hand blender on a low speed, blend the remaining chunks in the soup pot.

7 Add the salt, pepper, and nutmeg to season and serve.

TIME	METHOD	SERVES
2 Hours 30 Minutes	Stove Top	4 People

POCAHONTAS
MEEKO'S FAVORITE SUCCOTASH SALSA AND CORN CHIPS

INGREDIENTS

- 16 oz rosa tomatoes, diced
- 1 can lima beans, drained
- 1 can whole-kernel yellow corn, drained
- ½ cup sweet onion, chopped
- ¼ cup olive oil
- 3 tbsp chopped parsley
- 3 tbsp white wine vinegar
- 1 tsp Himalayan salt
- ¾ tsp ground black pepper
- Your favourite corn chips

DIRECTIONS

1 Stir all of the ingredients together in a mixing bowl and drizzle over olive oil as well as the salt and pepper to taste

2 Serve with corn chips.

CHEF'S TIPS

- Add a side of vegan sour cream (like tofutti) to dip your corn chips into before adding the salsa.

TIME	SERVES
5 minutes	4 People

POCAHONTAS
JOHN SMITH'S MASHED POTATOES AND GRAVY

CHEF'S TIPS

- *The leftover mash from this recipe can be used to make potato fritters. Make patties out of the mash and fry with oil in a hot skillet. And, voila!*

INGREDIENTS

FOR THE POTATOES:

- *1.5 lbs russet potatoes, diced*
- *4 -5 cups water*
- *½ cup dairy free milk*
- *¼ cup vegan butter*
- *½ tsp garlic powder*
- *salt and pepper to taste*

FOR THE GRAVY:

- *⅓ cup cornstarch*
- *4-5 cups water*
- *2 tbsp vegetable stock powder*
- *⅛ tsp vegetable seasoning*
- *⅛ tsp white pepper*
- *pepper to taste*

TIME
40 minutes

METHOD
Stove Top

SERVES
4 People

DIRECTIONS

1. Place the potatoes into a large pot on the stove and cover with water. Place on a high heat and bring to a boil.

2. Make the gravy while the potatoes are boiling. Mix the cornstarch and ½ cup of water together in a bowl.

3. Continue to stir until there are no lumps and the cornstarch has dissolved.

4. In a small saucepan, mix the stock powder, 3 cups of water, vegetable spice and white pepper together. Place on a medium heat and stir continuously. As the gravy begins to thicken, add the pepper.

5. Once the mixture starts to boil, reduce the heat to low. This is now ready until serving.

6. When the potatoes are cooked through, remove them from the pot and drain them in a colander.

7. Place the potatoes back in their pot and add the vegan butter and ¼ cup of the dairy free milk.

8. Use a masher to soften and separate the potatoes. Add an additional ¼ cup of milk and continue to mash the potatoes until there are no lumps and you have a smooth mash consistency.

9. Stir in the garlic powder, salt and pepper. Serve with gravy. Enjoy!

JASMINE'S BUTTER CAULIFLOWER OVER RICE

INGREDIENTS

FOR THE CAULIFLOWER:

- ½ teaspoon garam masala
- ¼ teaspoon ground ginger
- ¼ teaspoon chili powder
- ¼ teaspoon curry powder
- 3 - 4 cups cauliflower florets
- 2 tbsp coconut milk
- 3 tsp coconut oil

FOR THE BUTTER SAUCE:

- 1 ½ tbsp coconut oil
- 1 small onion, chopped
- 1 tbsp garam masala
- ½ tsp chili powder
- ½ tsp ground black pepper
- 1 tsp curry powder
- 1 tsp sea salt
- 1 can coconut milk
- 6 ounces tomato paste
- 1 tablespoon fresh lime juice

DIRECTIONS

1. Place the cauliflower and all other accompanying ingredients (except for the oil) into a large bowl. Allow to sit and marinate for 20 minutes.

2. Heat the oil in a pan and add the cauliflower. Stir cauliflower and allow to cook until all sides of the florets start to brown. Set aside to cool.

3. Heat the coconut oil in a saucepan and add the onions and fry until translucent.

4. Stir in the garam masala, chili powder, sea salt, pepper and curry powder and cook until fragrances release (approximately 30 seconds).

5. Add the coconut milk and tomato paste, stirring frequently.

6. Increase heat and bring to a brief boil and then reduce to a simmer to allow the mixture to thicken.

7. Gently stir in the cauliflower and reduce heat to a low simmer. Cook for 5 minutes to allow cauliflower to absorb the flavors. Serve with naan bread or over basmati rice.

TIME	METHOD	SERVES
1 Hour	Oven	4 People

ALADDIN
ALADDIN'S NAAN AND HUMMUS FLATBREAD

INGREDIENTS

- 1 Naan flatbread
- 1 tsp olive oil
- ½ tsp and ¼ tsp spice mix (oregano, thyme, marjoram)
- 2 artichokes hearts from a can
- 1 tbsp chopped Kalamata olives
- 6 rosa tomatoes, chopped
- ½ cup cucumber, chopped into slices
- 2-3 mini bell peppers, roughly chopped
- 2 tsp red onion, finely chopped
- 2 tsp lemon juice, fresh
- ¼ cup hummus
- 2 tbsp chopped parsley
- 2 tbsp vegan feta cheese

CHEF'S TIPS

- *The toppings on this pizza can be interchanged with your plant based and veggie favorites.*

DIRECTIONS

1. Preheat the oven or oven to 400 Fahrenheit.

2. Prepare a baking tray with baking paper and non stick pray. Lightly brush the naan bread with oil and sprinkle for ½ tsp of the spice mix.

3. In the meanwhile, mix the artichokes, kalamata olives, tomatoes, cucumber. Peppers and red onion in a small bowl.

4. Stir in the spice mix and lemon juice.

5. Spread an even layer of hummus over the naan bread and layer with vegetables. Sprinkle vegan cheese on top.

6. Bake flatbread for approximately minutes until golden and crisp on the edges. This time may vary based on your oven. .

7. Sprinkle parsley over the flatbread to garnish

8. Cut into even slides with a pizza cutter and enjoy.

TIME	METHOD	SERVES
30 minutes	*Oven*	*2 People*

BEAUTY AND THE BEAST
BELLE'S TEA TIME CHOCOLATE CHOUX BUNS

TIME	METHOD	SERVES
45 minutes	*Oven*	*6 People*

CHEF'S TIPS

- *The toppings on this pizza can be interchanged with your plant based and veggie favorites.*

INGREDIENTS

FOR THE DONUT PROFITEROLES:

- *½ cup dairy free milk*
- *5 tbsp vegan butter*
- *2 cups all-purpose flour*
- *2 tsp baking powder*
- *⅛ tsp salt*
- *½ cup powdered sugar*
- *6⅓ cups vegetable oil, for frying*

FOR THE CREAMY FILLING:

- *1⅓ cups coconut cream*
- *1½ ounces Baileys liqueur*
- *1 tsp vanilla bean paste*
- *2 tbsp powdered sugar*
- *For the chocolate sauce:*
- *1¼ cups dairy free milk*
- *3 tbsp agave nectar*
- *3½ ounces vegan dark chocolate, finely chopped*

DIRECTIONS

1 Add the milk and butter to a saucepan on medium heat and stir until butter is melted.

2 Whisk the flour, baking powder, powdered sugar and salt together in a mixing bowl.

3 Stir in the milk and butter mixture until you have a dough like consistency.

4 Lightly dust your work surface with flour and scoop two tablespoons of dough into your hands and roll to form a ball. Repeat with the rest of the dough.

5 Prepare a baking tray with baking paper and non-stick spray.

6 Preheat your deep-fryer to 340 degrees Fahrenheit.

7 Place 4 balls at a time in the deep fryer and fry for approximately 3-4 minutes until they become golden brown.

8 Fry 4 balls at a time for 4 minutes, or until golden brown.

9 Scoop the balls out of the oil and place on a paper towel to cool.

10 For the creamy filling, whisk all of the ingredients together in a bowl until you have a stiffer, cream like consistency. Set aside until you are ready to serve.

11 To make the chocolate sauce, place a saucepan on medium heat and add the milk and agave.

12 In a mixing bowl, add the chocolate and pour the warmed milk mixture over. Stir until the chocolate is completely melted.

13 Cut profiteroles in half lengthwise. Pipe generous amounts of cream on bottom halves and sandwich with top halves.

14 Before serving, in a heavy-based pan, melt sugar until golden.

15 Drizzle this over the stack of profiteroles before adding the chocolate sauce. Drizzle with chocolate sauce and serve.

103

GASTON'S PAN BAGNAT SANDWICH

INGREDIENTS

- White beans (either butter or cannellini beans)
- Red bell pepper, sliced
- Kalamata olives
- Artichoke hearts –from a can, drained
- Red onion, chopped
- Dijon mustard
- Lemon juice
- Extra virgin Olive oil
- Freshly baked baguettes
- Tomatoes
- Basil + parsley
- Salt + pepper

CHEF'S TIPS

- Try adding capers to the sandwich mix for an extra tangy taste.

DIRECTIONS

1 In a small bowl, mix dijon mustard, oil oil and lemon juice together until the dijon is emulsified.

2 In a large mixing bowl, add the beans. Use the back of a fork to roughly mash the beans. Stir in the dressing mix well.

3 Add in the pepper, artichokes, red onion, olives, parsley and salt & pepper. Mix well.

4 Cut bread in half lengthwise and brush both halves lightly with olive oil.

5 Spread a layer of the mixed salad to the bottom half of the bread with a good serving of the mixed salad.

6 Add tomatoes, basil leaves and salt & pepper. Cover with the other baguette.

7 Wrap sandwich tightly sandwich wrap and place in the fridge overnight.

8 Serve chilled or at room temperature. Makes 2 sandwiches

TIME	METHOD	SERVES
15 minutes	Oven	2 People

BEAUTY AND THE BEAST
THE BEAST'S HEARTY FRENCH ONION SOUP

INGREDIENTS

- ¼ cup vegan butter
- 4 yellow onions, chopped
- 1 ½ tsp dried thyme
- 2 bay leaves
- ½ tsp salt
- 1 tbsp flour
- ¾ cup dry white wine
- 6 cup vegetable stock
- ½ tsp pepper
- 1 baguette, sliced
- vegan mozzarella

CHEF'S TIPS

If you prefer to keep the soup as it is, toast the baguettes separately and add some vegan butter instead of adding them into the soup.

DIRECTIONS

1 Slice the onions lengthwise after removing the ends and out layer.

2 Using a deep, large pot, heat the butter over medium heat and add the onions, thyme, bay leaves and salt to taste.

3 Cook the onions for 45 minutes on a low to medium heat to allow them to caramelize.

4 Sprinkle in the flour and stir until you have no more white patches..

5 Slowly pour in the vegan wine and stir continuously to allow the wine to reduce. This should take approximately 10 minutes.

6 Now stir in the vegetable stock and increase the heat to bring the pot to a boil. Once boiling reduce the heat to allow the pot to simmer for 30 minutes.

7 Spoon the soup into four serving bowls which are oven proof. Preheat the oven to 350 degrees Fahrenheit. Place a slice of baguette on top of each bowl of soup and sprinkle with the vegan cheese on top.

8 Place the bowls in the oven and allow the cheese time to melt. Once it starts to go a golden brown, remove the bowls from the oven and serve!

TIME	METHOD	SERVES
60 minutes	*Stove Top / Oven*	*4 People*

THE HUNCHBACK OF NOTRE DAME
ESMERALDA'S TOPSY TURVY UPSIDE-DOWN CAKE

INGREDIENTS

- 2 Pears , thinly sliced
- 3 tbsp maple syrup

WET INGREDIENTS:

- ¾ cup dairy free milk
- ¼ cup applesauce
- 1 tbsp lemon juice
- ⅓ cup sugar
- ¼ cup cooking oil
- 1 tsp vanilla essence
- 1 tsp cinnamon

DRY INGREDIENTS:

- 1.5 cups all-purpose flour
- 2 tsp baking powder
- ¼ tsp baking soda
- ½ tsp salt

DIRECTIONS

1. Preheat the oven to 350 degrees Fahrenheit.

2. Line a 9 inch cake pan with baking paper at the bottom.

3. Arrange pear slices evenly across the bottom. Drizzle the maple syrup over the pear slices.

4. Place the remaining pieces of pear in a blender with 1 teaspoon of water and blend until you have an applesauce like consistency.

5. Set aside ¼ cup of the puree to use in the cake.

6. Stir all of the wet ingredients together in a large mixing bowl until well combined.

7. Mix all the dry ingredients together in a separate bowl. Slowly stir in 1 ¼ cups flour to the wet mixture. Continue to add 1-2 tablespoons at a time until you have a slightly stiffer mixture.

8. Pour this mixture into the cake pan over the pear slices and spread evenly.

9. Bake for 40 minutes and then allow to cool for 15 minutes before turning the cake out of the pan. Slowly peel away the baking paper.

10. Sprinkle cinnamon on the pears. Slice, serve and enjoy!

TIME	METHOD	SERVES
1 hour 15 minutes	Oven	8 People

THE HUNCHBACK OF NOTRE DAME
QUASIMODO'S POTATO LEEK SOUP

INGREDIENTS

6 medium potatoes, cut into
cubes
1 leek, chopped into thin
slices
1 tsp garlic powder
2 tsp salt
1 bay leaf
1 ½ tsp tarragon
1 ½ dried thyme
1 tsp dried rosemary
Pinch of pepper
4 cups of water

CHEF'S TIPS

*Serve this dish with a
slice of bread or baguette*

DIRECTIONS

1. Heat the oil. Butter and a pinch of salt in a large pot on the stove.

2. Add in the leeks and onion and fry until both become translucent.

3. Add in the potatoes, crushed garlic and other spices and sauce for 3 to four minutes.

4. Pour in the vegetable stock and add the bay leaf along with the salt and pepper. Turn up the heat so that the pot can simmer and cook for 20 minutes.

5. Once the potatoes are tender, remove from the heat and scoop out the bay leaves.

6. Stir in the coconut milk and add in the lemon juice to taste.

7. Use a hand held blender to pulse the soup until you have a smooth mixture.

TIME	METHOD	SERVES
60 minutes	*Stove Top*	*6 People*

SLEEPING BEAUTY
PRINCESS AURORA'S BIRTHDAY CAKE

TIME	METHOD	SERVES
60 minutes	Oven	8 People

CHEF'S TIPS

Add your favorite sprinkles to the top of the cake before serving.

INGREDIENTS

FOR THE CAKE:

- *6 cups all-purpose flour*
- *2 ⅛ cups coconut sugar*
- *3 ½ tsp baking powder*
- *1 ¾ tsp baking soda*
- *½ tsp finely ground sea salt*
- *2 ½ cup dairy free milk*
- *3 ½ tsp apple cider vinegar*
- *1 ¼ cup unsweetened applesauce*
- *½ cup coconut oil, melted*
- *3 ½ tbsp vanilla extract*

FOR THE FROSTING:

- *4 cups vegan butter*
- *7 cups powdered sugar*
- *1 tbsp vanilla essence*
- *2–3 tbsp dairy-free milk*
- *2 tsp blue food coloring*

DIRECTIONS

1 Preheat the oven to 350F and spray two 8 inch cake pans and two 6 inch cake pans with nonstick spray and line with baking paper.

2 In a small mixing bowl, stir the apple cider vinegar to the milk and set aside to sour.

3 In a large mixing bowl, whisk the flour, sugar baking powder, baking soda and salt together.

4 In a medium bowl, mix the sour milk, coconut oil, applesauce, and vanilla essence together.

5 Slowly add the wet ingredients to the dry and stir until you have a smooth batter.

6 Divide the batter evenly into the four cake pans and place in the oven - 25 mins for the 6 inch and 30 mins for 8 inch pans.
Set the cakes aside to cool while you make the frosting.
In a large bowl, beat the butter until creamy and slowly add the powdered sugar. Once added, stir in 2 T of milk and the vanilla essence.

7 Place each baked cake on their own plate.

8 Starting with one of the 8 inch cakes, spread frosting along the top and sides. Place the second 8 inch on top and repeat followed by each of the 6 inch cakes. Place in the fridge.

9 Once you've finished creating the tiers, make sure they are all chilling in the fridge (at least 10 minutes).

10 Now you'll make the vegan blue buttercream. Add in the blue plant based food dye to the bowl and use a hand mixer to evenly distribute the color. Prepare the piping tip and spoon the buttercream into the piping bag. Place the piping bag into the fridge to chill as well.

11 Build the cake by laying the bigger cake layers at the bottom followed by the smaller layers. While adding each layer, using the piping bag to ice in between each layer.

12 Add the candles and serve.

SLEEPING BEAUTY
MALEFICENT'S MIDNIGHT BLACK PANCAKES

INGREDIENTS

- 1 ½ cups all-purpose flour
- 1 ½ tsp baking powder
- 2 tbsp coconut sugar
- 3 ½ tbsp coconut oil
- 2 tsp activated charcoal
- 1 cup dairy free milk
- 1 flax egg

CHEF'S TIPS

- Top with blueberries and blackberries before serving.
- One Flax egg is made with 1 tbsp ground flax seeds to 3 tbsp water.

DIRECTIONS

1 Whisk all the ingredients together to create a batter.

2 Place a pan on medium heat with some oil and spoon in a large tablespoon of batter to create each pancake. Cook and both sides.

3 Repeat until all the batter is used.

4 Serve and enjoy!

TIME	METHOD	SERVES
15 minutes	Stove Top	4 People

MOTHER GOTHEL'S HAZELNUT (AND PARSNIP) SOUP

INGREDIENTS

- 3 tbsp vegan butter or coconut oil
- 1 small onion, diced
- 2 tsp crushed garlic
- 1 tsp dried thyme
- ¼ small apple, sliced
- 1 lbs parsnips, sliced
- 4 cups vegetable stock
- ¼ tsp cardamom
- ⅛ tsp white pepper
- ½ cup vegan cream,
- Salt to taste

CHEF'S TIPS

Serve in bowls with crushed toasted hazelnuts. A little drizzle of hazelnut oil is nice if you have it too. Top with a thyme sprig. Enjoy!

DIRECTIONS

1 Place a large pot on the stove and heat the butter or coconut oil on a medium heat. Add in the onions and fry them until they soften and become translucent.

2 Now add the apples, garlic and dried thyme. Fry and stir until the spices become fragrant.

3 Add in the sliced parsnips and the salt to taste.

4 Turn up the heat and allow the bot to come to a boil. Once boiling, turn the heat down and place a lid on the pot.

5 Allow to simmer until the parsnips become soft. This will take between 10 to 15 minutes.

6 Remove the pot from the heat and, using a hand blender, pulse the mixture until you have a smooth consistency. Stir in the white pepper and cardamom followed by the vegan cream.

7 Serve hot and enjoy!

TIME	METHOD	SERVES
30 minutes	*Stove Top*	*4 People*

TANGLED
RAPUNZEL'S STUFFED GOLDEN SPAGHETTI SQUASH

INGREDIENTS

- 1 spaghetti squash
- 1 tbsp cooking oil
- 1 tsp crushed garlic
- 7 Oz baby spinach
- ⅔ cup cashew cream
- Salt to taste
- Pepper to taste
- 1 cup vegan feta cheese
- ¾ vegan cheese

CHEF'S TIPS

- Serve with Parmesan (vegan) and pine nuts.

DIRECTIONS

1 Preheat the oven to 400 degrees Fahrenheit

2 Cut the squash lengthwise and scoop out any seeds

3 Drizzle the cooking oil over the squash and place them facing down on a prepared oven dish.

4 Bake the squash for 40 minutes or until it is easy to prick with a sharp knife. Once cooked, set aside while you make the spinach cream.

5 Place a small saucepan on the stove and add some cooking oil. Add the crushed garlic followed by the spinach.

6 Once the spinach has wilted, stir in the cashew cream. Add salt and pepper to taste.

7 Scoop the spinach cream into each squash and place and sprinkle some vegan cheese over before placing in the oven for 3 minutes.

8 Serve hot and enjoy!

TIME	METHOD	SERVES
50 minutes	Oven	2 People

TARZAN
TERK & TANTOR'S PEANUT BUTTER AND BANANA BREAKFAST COOKIES

INGREDIENTS

WET INGREDIENTS:

- 2 ripe bananas
- ½ cup sugar and salt free peanut butter
- 2 tbsp maple syrup
- 2 tbsp coconut oil
- 2 flax eggs
- 1 tsp vanilla essence

DRY INGREDIENTS:

- 2 cups oats
- ½ tsp baking soda
- ½ tsp baking powder

CHEF'S TIPS

- Add in your favourite chopped seeds or dried fruit to the recipe to match your taste buds.
- Mix 1 T ground flaxseed with 3 T of water to make one egg

DIRECTIONS

1 Preheat the oven to 325°Fahrenheit. Prepare a baking tray by lining it with baking paper and spray with a non stick spray.

2 Add the ripe bananas to a large bowl and mash them using the back of a fork.

3 Add the remaining wet ingredients to the banana and mix until well combined.

4 Now fold in all of the dry ingredients.

5 Using a big spoon, scoop out a portion of the dough and form into your desired shape and size. Repeat with all remaining dough.

6 Place each cookie onto the baking tray and space evenly.
Bake for 10 minutes or until the cookies slowly brown.
Allow the cookies to cool completely before serving.

TIME	METHOD	SERVES
20 minutes	Oven	4 People

TARZAN
JANE'S JUNGLE CURRY

INGREDIENTS

- 1 tbsp coconut oil
- 1 packet firm tofu
- 2 tbsp green or red curry paste (depending on how spicy you would like your curry to be)
- 1 small aubergine, cut into cubes
- ½ cup mushrooms,
- 150 g of bamboo shoots
- 2 cups vegetable stock
- 1 tbsp vegan fish sauce
- 2 tbsp maple syrup
- 1 sprig fresh basil
- 3 cups rice, cooked

CHEF'S TIPS

- The tofu in this recipe can be replaced with firm tempeh cut into cubes.

DIRECTIONS

1 Place a wok or deep pot on a medium heat and add the coconut oil. Tilt the wok or pan to ensure the oil is spread across the inside surface.

2 Add the tofu and fry on each side until each side becomes a slightly golden brown. Be careful not to burn the tofu as this can be easy to do when frying it in a thin wok on a high heat.

3 Add the mushrooms, eggplant and bamboo shoots. Stir in the water, fish sauce, curry paste and sugar.

4
5 Place a lid on the wok and allow to boil. Reduce the heat to a low and let simmer for approximately 30 minutes.

6 Remove the wok from the stove and add the basil leaves. Serve over the rice and enjoy!

TIME	METHOD	SERVES
50 minutes	Oven	4 People

STAR WARS
PRINCESS LEIA OUT OF THIS WORLD CINNAMON BUNS

TIME	METHOD	SERVES
60 minutes	*Oven*	*6 People*

INGREDIENTS

FOR THE DOUGH:

- 2 cups dairy free milk - at room temperature
- ½ cup vegan butter
- ¼ cup brown sugar
- 1 tsp dry yeast
- 5 ½ cups all-purpose flour
- 1 tsp salt

FOR THE FILLING:

- ¾ cup vegan butter
- ¾ cup brown sugar
- 2 tbsp ground cinnamon

FOR THE ICING:

- 1 cup powdered sugar
- 2 tbsp dairy free milk
- ½ tsp vanilla essence

DIRECTIONS

1. Spray two oven pans with nonstick spray.
2. Melt the butter in a microwave for a few seconds. Whisk the milk, butter and sugar together in a bowl. You want the mixture to be just warm.
3. Add the yeast and let the mixture sit for 1 to 2 minutes.
4. Stir in the 5 cups of flour and the salt and stir until well combined.
5.
6. Place a clean tea towel over the top of the bowl and allow the dough time to rise - 1 hour.
7. Preheat the oven to 350 degrees Fahrenheit.
8. After your dough has risen, add an additional ½ cup of flour and salt.
9. Sprinkle some flour over your working surface and start to knead the dough using your Knead using your hands. If your dough is still very sticky, add some additional flour.
10. Using a rolling pin, roll the dough out to form a rectangle. You want the dough to be approximately ½ inch thick.
11. Spread the butter over the surface over the dough and sprinkle with the sugar and cinnamon.
12. Starting on one end of the rectangle, roll the dough to form a log and pinch each end closed. Roll the dough log so that the seam side is on the underneath.
13. Cut the dough log in half and then further cut each half into 7 even pieces. Place 7 rolls in each of the baking pans and cover to allow the dough to rise for a further 30 minutes.
14. While the dough is rising, make the frosting. Whisk the sugar, almond milk and vanilla essence together.
15. Place the dough rolls into the oven for 30 minutes or until they start becoming a golden brown color. Remove from the oven and drizzle with the frosting. Serve warm and enjoy!

STAR WARS
QUEEN AMIDALA GALAXY FAR FAR AWAY CUPCAKES

TIME	METHOD	SERVES
40 minutes	*Oven*	*6 People*

INGREDIENTS

FOR THE CUPCAKES:

- 2 cups dairy free milk
- 1 T apple cider vinegar
- 2 ½ cups all-purpose flour
- ⅔ cup cocoa powder
- ½ T baking soda
- 1 tsp baking powder
- ⅔ cup cooking oil
- 1 ½ cups sugar
- 2 tsp vanilla essence
- 3 vegan candy bars (similar to a milky way bar)

FOR THE GALAXY FROSTING:

- ¾ cup organic whipped earth balance
- ¾ cup vegan butter
- 1 T vanilla essence
- 4 ½ cups powdered sugar
- 4 T cocoa powder
- 4 varieties of vegan food coloring

DIRECTIONS

1. Preheat the oven to 350 degrees Fahrenheit
2. Prepare 2 cupcake plans with cupcake wrappers and non-stick spray.
3. Line 2 cupcake pans with cupcake liners.
4. Cut the candy cars up into rectangular pieces
5. Mix the apple cider vinegar and dairy free milk. Set aside for the milk to sour.
6. Mix the flour, cocoa powder, baking soda and baking powder together.
7. Stir the oil, sugar and vanilla into the sour milk mixture and stir well.
8. Now stir in all of the dry ingredients slowly to the wet until well combined.
9. Pour the mixture evenly into each cupcake wrapper, filling each approximately halfway.
10. Press a piece of rectangular candy bar into the middle of each cupcake.
11. Place the oven and bake for 15-18 minutes depending on the strength of your oven. Set aside and allow to cool while you make the icing.
12. Leave the ingredients sitting out before using them. Best results come from using room temperature ingredients.
13. Using a handheld mixer, mix the earth balance and vegan butter together until you have a creamy mixture. Slowly add the powdered sugar and continue to mix. Now add the vanilla essence.
14. Divide this icing mix into four separate bowls.
15. Divide the frosting into 4 bowls and add a color of your choice of food coloring to each bowl.
16. Spoon each color into an icing piping bag and place these four into a larger piping bag. Pipe swirls of frosting onto each cupcake.

116

STAR WARS
CHEWBACCA CHILI

INGREDIENTS

- 1 T cooking oil
- 1 onion, diced
- 1 cup carrots, shredded
- 1-2 chillies, finely chopped
- 2 tsp crushed garlic
- ½ cup bulgur wheat
- 2 T chili powder
- 1 T ground cumin
- 2 cups diced fresh tomatoes
- 1 ½ cups tomato sauce
- 1 can kidney beans
- 1 ½ cans black beans
- 1 ½ tsp salt
- Fresh cilantro, chopped

CHEF'S TIPS

- Sprinkle with vegan cheese, or a dollop of vegan sour cream before serving

DIRECTIONS

1 Place a large pot on the stove and add the cooking oil on medium heat.

2 Add the onion, carrots, chillies and fry until the onion starts to soften and becomes translucent.

3 Sir in the garlic followed by the bulgur wheat, chili powder and cumin.

4 Once the spices start to become fragrant, stir in the canned tomatoes, tomato sauce and the beans.

5 Increase to a high heat and allow the bot to come to boil. Reduce the heat and allow it to simmer.

6 The chili will need approximately an hour to simmer on a low heat to allow for enough time for the spices to be absorbed throughout the dish.

7 Add salt to taste and sprinkle with cilantro when just before serving.

TIME	METHOD	SERVES
30 minutes	Stove Top	4 People

STAR WARS
THE CHILD MATCHA GREEN TEA LATTE

INGREDIENTS

- 1 ¼ tsp matcha powder
- 1 tbsp maple syrup
- 1 tbsp boiling water
- ¾ cup coconut milk, a lite version
- ¾ cup macadamia nut milk

CHEF'S TIPS

- *Add in maca root powder to give a healthy boost to your tea latte.*

DIRECTIONS

1 Grab your favorite drinking mug and add the matcha powder to it along with a sweetener of your choice.

2 Add matcha powder to your serving mug along with a sweetener of choice and the boiling water. and hot water.
Stir briskly until the matcha is completely dissolved.

3 Whisk with a bamboo whisk or a metal whisk until completely dissolved.

4 Gently heat the coconut and macadamia milk using a milk frother or over the stove.

5 Add the milk mixture to the matcha in your mug. Taste the drink and add the maple syrup to sweeten the drink if needed.

6 Serve immediately and enjoy!

TIME	METHOD	SERVES
5 Minutes	*Stove Top*	*1 Person*

WRECK-IT RALPH

VANELLOPE VON SCHWEETZ STRAWBERRY BANANA ICE CREAM SUNDAE

INGREDIENTS

- *1 cup fresh raspberries*
- *1 ½ tbsp of maple syrup*
- *coconut nectar*
- *½ tsp of pure vanilla essence*
- *Fresh mint*
- *4 large bananas, ripe - frozen overnight*
- *1 tsp vanilla essence*
- *Fresh strawberries to garnish*
- *Vegan Strawberry Syrup like Hershey's*

DIRECTIONS

1 Using a blender, add the raspberries, maple syrup and vanilla essence and pulse until you have a smooth mixture.

2 Add in the mint and pulse a few times.

3 Chop the frozen bananas and add to a blender or food processor until the banana is crumbly.

4 Make sure to use a spatula and scrape down the sides of the blender to ensure the entire mixture is being blended.

5 Pour in the vanilla essence and pulse again until you have an ice cream like consistency.

6 Add two scoops to a serving bowl and drizzle with the raspberry mixture. Garnish with some fresh mint and fresh strawberries.

TIME
15 minutes

SERVES
1 Person

WRECK-IT RALPH
NO BAKE SUGAR RUSH MINT BROWNIES

INGREDIENTS

FOR THE BROWNIE LAYER:

- *1 cup pitted dates, soaked and soft*
- *2 tsp coconut oil*
- *Pinch of salt*
- *1 cup walnuts*
- *½ cup rolled oats*
- *3 tbsp cocoa powder*
- *¼ cup dark chocolate chips*
- *1 mint candy cane, crushed*

FOR THE MINT GANACHE LAYER:

- *⅓ cup coconut milk, full cream*
- *¾ tsp peppermint essence*
- *½ cup dark chocolate chips*

FOR THE CANDY CANE TOPPING:

- *1-2 mint candy canes, crushed*

DIRECTIONS

1 Pulse the walnuts and oats in a food processor until you have a rough flour like mixture. Add to a small bowl and set aside.

2 Add the soft dates, coconut oil and pinch of salt and pulse in your food processor until you have a paste like consistency.

3 Sprinkle in the cocoa, walnut & oat flour mix, chocolate chips and the crushed candy cane. Pulse again until this brownie mixture is thoroughly combined.

4 Prepare a loaf pan by spraying it with nonstick spray and lining it with baking paper.

5 Add the brownie mixture and press it into the corners and sides of the pan until it is evenly layered. Place in the freezer will you complete the ganache.

6 Using a double boiler, fill the bottom boiler halfway with hot water and bring to the boil.

7 In the top half of the boiler, pour in the coconut milk and mint essence to the bowl followed by the chocolate chips. Make sure not to burn this mixture. Once the chocolate chips are melted, remove from the stove and give it a quick stir.

8 Pour this mixture over the brownies and add back to the freezer for 20 minutes. Remove from freezer, cut into squares and serve!

TIME	METHOD	SERVES
45 minutes	*Stove Top*	*12 People*

WRECK-IT RALPH
RALPH'S CRUNCHY CRISPY RICE CHOCOLATE BLOCKS

INGREDIENTS

- 2 cups Rice Krispies cereal
- ⅓ cup white sesame seeds
- 1 ¼ cups vegan chocolate chips
- ¾ cup peanut butter
- ⅓ cup coconut oil
- ⅓ cup maple syrup
- 1 tsp instant coffee

CHEF'S TIPS
- Add chopped almonds to this recipe for extra crunch

DIRECTIONS

1 Prepare a brownie baking tin with baking paper and spray with nonstick spray.

2 Place the cereal and sesame seeds into a large mixing bowl and set aside.

3 Melt the chocolate chips, peanut butter, coconut oil, maple syrup and instant coffee in a small bowl in the microwave.
Stir the chocolate mixture using a spatula into the dry ingredients and mix until well combined.

4 Pour this mixture into a baking tray and spread evenly.
Place into the fridge and allow to set for 2 hours.
Once the chocolate block is solid, slice into bars and serve.

5 Chill uncovered in the fridge for 1 to 1 and 1/2 hours or until VERY firm. Slice into bars and enjoy! Recipe yields 16-32 bars depending on how big you want them! Enjoy!!

TIME	METHOD	MAKES
1 Hour 30 Minutes	Refrigerator	20 Bars

121

JAMES AND THE GIANT PEACH

JAMES PEACH COBBLER

INGREDIENTS

- 2 cans of sliced peaches
- ¼ cup granulated sugar
- 1 tbsp cornstarch
- ½ cup vegan butter
- ¾ cup granulated sugar
- 1 tsp vanilla essence
- 1 tbsp dairy free milk
- 1 cup all-purpose flour
- 1 tsp baking powder
- ⅛ tsp salt

CHEF'S TIPS

- If peaches aren't your favorite fruit, replace them with tinned pears.

DIRECTIONS

1. Preheat the oven to 350 degrees Fahrenheit.

2. Prepare a 8 inch by 8 inch dish by lining it with baking paper and a thin coat of nonstick spray.

3. Layer the sliced peaches and sprinkle with the ¼ cup of granulated sugar and cornstarch.

4. Use a spoon to mix the peaches with the sugar and cornstarch.

5. Mix the vegan butter (melted). ¾ cup of granulated sugar, vanilla and milk together until well combined. Slowly stir in the flour, baking powder and salt and mix to combine. This mix should be a dough like consistency.

6. Add the dough on top of the peaches and bake for 25 minutes.

7. Remove from the oven and scoop the peaches into a serving bowl. Add a scoop of ice cream and serve. Enjoy!

TIME	METHOD	SERVES
60 minutes	Oven	4 People

MONSTERS INC
MIKE'S SPICY SHIITAKE MUSHROOM SUSHI ROLLS

TIME	METHOD	SERVES
30 minutes	*Stove Tops*	*4 People*

INGREDIENTS

FOR THE RICE:

- *1 cup sushi rice*
- *1 cup water*
- *1 tsp rice vinegar*
- *1 tsp sugar*
- *½ tsp salt*

FOR THE MUSHROOMS:

- *2 cups diced king oyster mushrooms, soaked in warm water for 20 minutes*
- *½ cup water*
- *1 cup cornstarch*
- *Cooking oil*
- *For the sauce:*
- *½ cup vegan mayo*
- *1 tbsp sriracha*

TO ASSEMBLE:

- *4 toasted nori sheets*
- *4 tbsp sesame seeds*
- *1 ripe avocado, sliced*

PREPARATION

1. Cook the sushi rice on the stove according to the packet instructions. Once cooked, stir in the rice vinegar, sugar and salt. Set aside to cool.
2. Place a deep pot on the stove on a medium heat and add 2 inches of oil. Dip the shopped mushrooms into the cornstarch.
3. Once the oil is heated up, add a ¼ of the chopped mushrooms and mix them in the oil to coat and cook. Allow them to cook until they become golden brown.
4. Scoop out the cooked pieces of mushroom and place on paper towels to drain any excess oil.
5. Lay a bamboo mat flat and spread a sheet of nori over. Spread a thin layer of rice (¼ of the rice portion) over the nori. You may need to keep your hands wet to ensure the rice doesn't stick to your fingers. Sprinkle a tablespoon of sesame seeds over.
6. Mix the sauce ingredients together and pour over the mushrooms. Spread ¼ of the mushrooms over the rice evenly.
7. Roll the sushi away from you, adding slices of avocado as you roll. You will need to grip the bamboo mat tightly but gently so as not to squash the sushi.
8. Using a sharp knife, slice the roll into small but even pieces.
9. Repeat the above process 3 more times to finish the rice and mushroom ingredients.
10. Serve with pickled ginger and soy sauce and enjoy!

BOO'S FAVORITE AVOCADO GREEN MONSTER PASTA

INGREDIENTS

- 1 ¼ cup uncooked pasta
- 1 tsp crushed garlic
- 1/4 cup fresh basil leaves,
- 2 tbsp fresh lemon juice, to taste
- 1 tbsp extra-virgin olive oil
- 1 medium avocado, ripe
- 1 tbsp water
- Sea salt, to taste
- Black pepper, to taste
- Lemon zest, for serving

CHEF'S TIPS

- For a variation lower in calories, replace the regular pasta with zucchini noodles.

DIRECTIONS

1. Place a large pot of water on high heat and allow it to boil. Cook the pasta according to the packet instructions.

2. Make the avocado sauce while the pasta cooks. Add the garlic and basil to a food processor until you have a minced mixture.

3. Add the oil, avocado, lemon juice, oil, and 1 tablespoon water and pulse a few times until you have a smooth mixture. If the mixture is slightly too thick, add a few more drops of oil and pulse again.

4. Once the pasta is cooked, drain it in a colander and place it back in its pot. Stir in the avocado sauce until well combined. Add salt and pepper to taste.

5. If desired, serve with a garnish of basil leaves and lemon zest.

6. Enjoy!

TIME	METHOD	SERVES
30 minutes	Stove Top	4 People

SULLEY'S BLUE SPIRULINA SMOOTHIE

INGREDIENTS

FOR THE SMOOTHIE:

- *2 tbsp of blue spirulina*
- *2 medium bananas, frozen*
- *1 Cup peaches, frozen*
- *¼ cup pineapple, frozen*
- *1 Cup dairy free milk*

TOPPINGS:

- *1 tsp blueberries, frozen*
- *1 tsp blackberries, frozen*
- *1 tbsp Cocoa nibs*
- *¼ Banana sliced*

CHEF'S TIPS

- *Add in chia seeds for some extra iron to your diet.*

DIRECTIONS

1. Blend the frozen bananas and dairy free milk in a blender until smooth. Add the pineapple and peaches and blend on a low speed.

2. Sprinkle in the blue spirulina and give another mix on a low speed.

3. Pour the mixture into your favorite serving mug or bowl and add your favorite toppings.

TIME	METHOD	SERVES
30 minutes	*Blender*	*1 Person*

RANDALL'S BE MY PAL CUPCAKES

INGREDIENTS

FOR THE CUPCAKES:

- 1 ¾ cups all-purpose flour
- 1 cup granulated sugar
- 1 T baking powder
- ½ tsp salt
- ¾ cup dairy free milk
- ¼ cup + 1 tbsp cooking oil
- ¼ cup apple sauce
- ¼ cup water
- 2 tsp vanilla essence

FOR THE CREAMY FROSTING:

- 6 tbsp vegan butter, melted
- 2 ¼ cups powdered sugar
- 2 tsp dairy free milk
- 1 tsp vanilla essence

DIRECTIONS

1. Preheat the oven to 350 degrees Fahrenheit. Prepare a muffin tray (12) by adding baking wrappers and spraying with a nonstick spray.
2. Stir the flour, sugar, baking powder and salt together in a medium sized bowl.
3. Stir the dairy free milk, oil, apple sauce, water, and vanilla extract together in a separate bowl.
4. Whisk the wet ingredients into the dry until you have an even and smooth batter.
5. Pour the batter evenly between the 12 cupcake wrappers and bake for 20 minutes or until the muffins pass the toothpick test.
6. Once baked, remove from the oven and allow the cupcakes to cool completely. Now make the frosting.
7. Cream the vegan butter in a food processor by beating it on a medium speed for two minutes. Lower speed and sprinkle in the powdered sugar. You may need to scrape down the sides of the mixer to ensure all the ingredients are mixed together.
8. Once you have added the sugar, increase the speed of the processor and blend for 3 minutes. Turn down the speed again and the milk and vanilla essence. Mix until well combined.
9. Spread the frosting evenly over the cooled cupcakes.
10. Serve!

TIME	METHOD	MAKES
50 minutes	Oven	12 Cupcakes

LILO AND STITCH
STITCH AND LILO'S FAVORITE "HOUND DOG" SANDWICH

INGREDIENTS

- Two slices Texas Toast
- 1 medium banana, sliced
- 6 slices vegan bacon
- 3 tbsp peanut butter
- ¼ tbsp all-purpose flour
- ¼ cup dairy free milk
- 2 flax eggs
- 1 tbsp maple syrup
- A sprinkle of cinnamon, vanilla essence and sugar.

DIRECTIONS

1 Cook the bacon according to the packet instructions and set aside briefly.

2 To make the batter, stir the flour, milk and eggs together until well combined.

3 Place this batter in a medium sized pot on medium heat to warm up.

4 Dip and coat each piece of toast into the batter and add to a large saucepan to cook.

5 Make sure to watch each piece of toast carefully and flip regularly so that they do not burn.

6 Once the bacon and french toast are cooked, you are ready to assemble your hound dog sandwich.

7 Add the peanut butter, bananas, and bacon to once slice. Add the maple syrup and cover with a second slice of french toast.

8 Serve and enjoy!

TIME	METHOD	MAKES
30 minutes	Stove Top	1 Sandwich

CATRA AND ADORA'S ALMOND AND COCONUT RATION BARS

INGREDIENTS

- *1 cup almonds, chopped*
- *1 ¾ cups instant oats*
- *1 cup coconut flakes*
- *½ tsp ground cinnamon*
- *½ teaspoon salt*
- *1 cup peanut butter*
- *½ cup maple syrup*
- *1 ½ tsp vanilla essence*

CHEF'S TIPS
- *Maple syrup can be replaced with agave for a healthier option.*

PREPARATION

1 Prepare a 9 inch baking tin by lining it with baking paper and spraying with a non-stick spray.

2 Add a skillet or large frying pan to the stove and place on a medium heat. Add the almonds to toast them and stir continuously. The almonds should become fragrant and golden in colour.

3 Place the almonds in a mixing bowl and add the aots, coconut flakes, cinnamon and salt. Stir until well combined.

4 In a small bowl, add the peanut butter, maple syrup and vanilla essence and stir well.

5 Add this mixture to the dry ingredients and mix with a wooden spoon.

6 Add the mixture to the prepared baking tin and make sure it is evenly spread.

7 Cover the tin and place in the fridge for one hour to allow the coats to absorb the other ingredients.

8 Slice the bars into the width that you would like using a sharp knife. Serve and enjoy!

TIME	METHOD	MAKES
15 Minutes	*Oven*	*16 Bars*

ENCHANTED
GISELLE'S 'PEPPERONI' NEW YORK PIZZA

INGREDIENTS

FOR THE CRUST:

- 8 oz all-purpose flour
- ½ cup water
- 1 tbsp olive oil
- 2 tsp baking powder
- pinch salt

FOR THE SAUCE:

- 3 tbsp olive oil
- 1 ½ cup tomato sauce or paste
- ½ tsp dried basil
- 2 tsp dried oregano
- ½ tsp salt
- 1 tsp granulated sugar
- ¼ tsp black pepper (ground)

1/8 cup finely chopped onions

FOR THE TOPPINGS:

- 1 - 2 Cups vegan cheese
- Vegan Pepperonis (we recommend the lightlife brand)

PREPARATION

1 Pour olive oil into a saucepan on medium heat.

2 Add the onions and let cook until just starting to turn golden, stirring constantly for around 7 minutes.

3 Stir in the tomato sauce, salt, sugar, oregano, basil and pepper. (You can add a splash of red wine if you so desire)

4 Bring the sauce to a simmer. Then reduce heat to low; cover and allow to simmer until the flavors blend, (about 30 minutes).

5 Preheat the oven to 390 degree Fahrenheit.

6 Mix all the dough ingredients together and knead well until you have a slightly moist and sticky dough.

7 Flour your working surface and roll out the dough until you have a pizza dough which is to your desired thickness.

8 Spread the tomato paste on top of the crust with a ladel. Add the pepperoni slices and sprinkle over the vegan cheese.

9 Bake in the oven for 12-20 minutes. Take out of oven and allow the pizza to cool for 5 minutes. Slice and enjoy!

TIME	METHOD	SERVES
45 minutes	Oven	2 People

NOTES

NOTES

NOTES

NOTES

NOTES

A Note from the Authors:

Our readers are very important to us!

That's why we would love for you to consider writing us an Amazon review, and give us your feedback of The Official Princesses and Friends Cookbook.

We truly hope you had as much fun reading it and re-creating the recipes as we did making it!

Consider joining our mailing list for a special bonus recipe from our previous book The Unofficial Harry Potter Cookbook For Vegans:

SIGN UP HERE:
https://mailchi.mp/a2210107f97d/free-harry-potter-vegan-recipe

OR Simply scan the QR Code below!